SMOKE & MIRRORS

A Comedy/Murder Mystery

by

Will Osborne & Anthony Herrera

AF531084

SAMUEL FRENCH, INC.

45 WEST 25TH STREET NEW YORK 10010

7623 SUNSET BOULEVARD HOLLYWOOD 90046

LONDON *TORONTO*

Copyright © 1991, 1993 by Will Osborne and Anthony Herrera

ALL RIGHTS RESERVED

CAUTION: Professionals and amateurs are hereby warned that SMOKE & MIRRORS is subject to a royalty. It is fully protected under the copyright laws of the United States of America, the British Commonwealth, including Canada, and all other countries of the Copyright Union. All rights, including professional, amateur, motion picture, recitation, lecturing, public reading, radio broadcasting, television, and the rights of translation into foreign languages are strictly reserved. In its present form the play is dedicated to the reading public only.

The amateur live stage performance rights to SMOKE & MIRRORS are controlled exclusively by Samuel French, Inc., and royalty arrangements and licenses must be secured well in advance of presentation. PLEASE NOTE that amateur royalty fees are set upon application in accordance with your producing circumstances. When applying for a royalty quotation and license please give us the number of performances intended, dates of production, your seating capacity and admission fee. Royalties are payable one week before the opening performance of the play to Samuel French, Inc., at 45 W. 25th Street, New York, NY 10010; or at 7623 Sunset Blvd., Hollywood, CA 90046, or to Samuel French (Canada), Ltd., 80 Richmond Street East, Toronto, Ontario, Canada M5C 1P1.

Royalty of the required amount must be paid whether the play is presented for charity or gain and whether or not admission is charged.

Stock royalty quoted on application to Samuel French, Inc.

For all other rights than those stipulated above, apply to Lois Berman, 240 W. 44th Street, New York, NY 10036.

Particular emphasis is laid on the question of amateur or professional readings, permission and terms for which must be secured in writing from Samuel French, Inc.

Copying from this book in whole or in part is strictly forbidden by law, and the right of performance is not transferable.

Whenever the play is produced the following notice must appear on all programs, printing and advertising for the play: "Produced by special arrangement with Samuel French, Inc."

Due authorship credit must be given on all programs, printing and advertising for the play.

ISBN 0 573 69390 0 Printed in U.S.A.

For Mary, with love
W.O.

For Basha Plewinska
and
In memory of Cleavon Little
A.H.

No one shall commit or authorize any act or omission by which the copyright of, or the right to copyright, this play may be impaired.

No one shall make any changes in this play for the purpose of production.

Publication of this play does not imply availability for performance. Both amateurs and professionals considering a production are ***strongly*** advised in their own interests to apply to Samuel French, Inc., for written permission before starting rehearsals, advertising, or booking a theatre.

No part of this book may be reproduced, stored in a retrieval system, or transmitted in any form, by any means, now known or yet to be invented, including mechanical, electronic, photocopying, recording, videotaping, or otherwise, without the prior written permission of the publisher.

IMPORTANT BILLING AND CREDIT REQUIREMENTS

All producers of SMOKE & MIRRORS *must* give credit to the Authors of the Play in all programs distributed in connection with performances of the Play and in all instances in which the title of the Play appears for purposes of advertising, publicizing or otherwise exploiting the Play and/or a production. The names of the Authors *must* also appear on a separate line, on which no other name appears, immediately following the title, and *must* appear in size of type not less than fifty percent the size of the title type.

Smoke & Mirrors was originally produced by Bell Mare Productions in October, 1991, in a twelve-city tour of the state of Mississippi. The production was directed by John Shearin, with sets by Larry Kadlec, lighting by Bert Foregger, and costumes by Natalie Leavenworth. The stage manager was Michael Parker; company manager was Dale Jackson. The play was performed with the following cast:

HAMILTON ORR................Anthony Herrera
CLARK ROBINSON.................Will Osborne
BARBARA ORR................Marilyn McIntyre
DEREK COBURN...............Patrick St. Esprit
SHERIFF LEROY LUMPKIN.......Jack Stevens

During its development in the year following the Mississippi tour, *Smoke & Mirrors* was also produced by Oldcastle Theatre Company in Bennington, Vermont; by Flat Rock Playhouse in Flat Rock, North Carolina; and by Caldwell Theatre Company in Boca Raton, Florida.

CHARACTERS

HAMILTON ORR, a Hollywood producer/director

BARBARA ORR, a publicist, Hamilton's wife

CLARK ROBINSON, a screenwriter

DEREK COBURN, a film star

LEROY P. LUMPKIN, the sheriff

TIME

The present.

PLACE

The living room of Governor Robert Tubbman's beach house on a private island seven miles off the Mississippi Gulf coast.

ACT I

SETTING: The living room of a large southern beach house. In the room are a fireplace, an overstuffed armchair, a sofa, a coffee table, a player piano, an antique oak gun case containing a variety of rifles and shotguns, and a desk. On the desk are several unpacked cardboard boxes, a liter of Russian vodka, and four packages of Fig Newtons; also a laptop computer and printer, which seem out of place in this genteel setting. Above the desk is a display case, containing only one of a pair of engraved, nickel plated commemorative revolvers.

AT RISE: The sound of WAVES and the occasional cry of a SEAGULL are heard outside. HAMILTON ORR, a powerful, handsome man in his forties, paces back and forth stage center. HE holds the other commemorative revolver in his right hand. HE stops pacing stage center, cocks the pistol, and puts it to his temple. His hand shakes. HE speaks with a heavy southern accent.

HAMILTON. I have become too polluted to live. (*His hand continues to shake. Suddenly HE slams the pistol down on the table.*) No! No, no, no! (*HE rushes to the window and calls out.*) I don't want to live any more! (*HE moves quickly to the table, snatches up the pistol, and again puts it to his temple.*) I have become too poisoned to live.

(FOOTSTEPS are heard coming up the steps outside. A WOMAN'S VOICE calls out.)

WOMAN'S VOICE. (*Offstage.*) Hamilton? Hamilton?

(HAMILTON looks at his watch, mutters, and hurriedly puts the pistol back in its case above the desk. HE moves to the computer and begins to type.
BARBARA ORR enters. SHE is an attractive woman; SHE is dressed in a neat, stylish traveling outfit and carries a large carry-on bag and one piece of hand luggage)

BARBARA. Oh, Hamilton! (*Indicating the foliage outside.*) Honeysuckle, buttercups, verbena, Spanish moss hanging like witches hair—it just oozes those southern kind of secrets! (*SHE drops her bags and rushes to give Hamilton a kiss.*) Hello, darling.

(HAMILTON brushes her off; from now on HE speaks without a trace of southern accent.)

HAMILTON. (*Concerned.*) Where's Clark? Didn't he make the flight?

BARBARA. He's sitting on the edge of the dock with his head between his knees.

HAMILTON. (*Chuckling.*) Sea sick? From the water taxi?

BARBARA. No, no ... just "gathering the power to his center."

HAMILTON. Wacko.

BARBARA. Well, darling, after Vicksburg he figures he's going to need all the help he can get.

HAMILTON. (*Goes back to his typing.*) So. How was your reunion? Any sparks? Any re-kindling of the old flames?

BARBARA. Hamilton, don't ... please, you promised.

HAMILTON. (*Innocently.*) No, no, no. I was just ... curious.

BARBARA. It was very cordial. We agreed that we could be good friends.

HAMILTON. Ah.

(HAMILTON hits a command on the computer, and, during the following dialogue, the PRINTER churns out a page. BARBARA surveys the room.)

BARBARA. Hamilton, this place is perfect—I mean, a whole island all to ourselves? You're incredible!

HAMILTON. Thank your new "best friend," Governor Bob. You know, it's amazing how generous politicians can be when there's an election coming up. Especially after you let them know you're going to pump fifteen million dollars into their state economy before the end of the fiscal year.

(HAMILTON rips the paper out of the printer and begins to read. BARBARA continues to explore the room, visualizing a publicity photo layout.)

BARBARA. I can't believe this is just Bob's "get away" place. You know, this would make a terrific two-page spread in *Premiere* ... (*SHE flips a switch on the player piano and a rousing honky-tonk piano TUNE fills the room.*) Oh, that's fabulous! (*SHE sits at the piano and pretends to play, having a wonderful time.*)

HAMILTON. Shut that damn thing off! I'm trying to concentrate.

BARBARA. (*Shuts off the piano.*) Oh. Genius at work. Excuse me. (*SHE picks up her luggage and starts to the stairs.*) Now, where's our room? I'm dying to get out of these airplane clothes.

HAMILTON. Second on the left. The one with the view.

BARBARA. And Clark's?

HAMILTON. Right across the hall.

(SHE gives him an inscrutable look and ascends the stairs. HAMILTON looks after her for a moment, then goes to the door and calls toward the beach.)

HAMILTON. Clark! Zip up your "power" and come in here! (*HAMILTON takes out a cigarette lighter and ignites the page from the computer. HE puts the burning paper into the fireplace, then sits at his desk.*)

(CLARK ROBINSON, a high strung man with a small suitcase, opens the door and glares at Hamilton. HE wears newly purchased beach clothing—the paper size tag is still sewn to the pocket of his Bermuda shorts.)

HAMILTON. Hello, Clark. (*HE gestures broadly to the room.*) Welcome to Fantasy Island.

CLARK. Okay. Okay. Wait a minute. (*HE sets down his bag and closes the door.*) Before we start I just want to say something. (*HE closes his eyes, stretches out his arms, and takes several quick breaths to "gather his power."*) Okay. Hamilton, I am no longer mad at you about Vicksburg. There. Okay? Okay. Now. That does not mean that I am not *angry* about Vicksburg. Oh yes. Yes. I am angry about Vicksburg. But I own that anger now. It is a part of my reality. Okay? And since that which does not kill us makes us stronger, and I am not dead, am I? No. Then I must be stronger because of ... Vicksburg. So. In a sense, I suppose I should thank you for Vicksburg. But I won't. And that's all I have to say.

HAMILTON. That's all you have to say?

CLARK. Yes.

HAMILTON. And you feel better now?

CLARK. Yes.

HAMILTON. Good. Would you like a Fig Newton?

CLARK. Yes. Very much. Thank you.

(HAMILTON holds out a pack of Fig Newtons to Clark. CLARK takes four or five of them and sits in the armchair.)

HAMILTON. (*Crossing to Clark.*) You know, Clark, I'm glad you brought up Vicksburg, because it's been on my mind, too. And—this is a little hard for me to say—but I think perhaps I owe you an apology.

(CLARK looks up.)

HAMILTON. Yes. I think maybe you were right about the final cut.

CLARK. I was?

HAMILTON. Well, it was never *my* idea to put the synthesizers behind Sherman's attack, you know that, and I don't think anyone could have talked Derek out of General Lee's fantasy montage with the buxom slave girl—

(CLARK reacts.)

HAMILTON. But maybe I should have fought a little harder to keep everything else more like the way you wrote it.

CLARK. Damn right you should have.

HAMILTON. *So* I apologize. But in the final analysis, Clark, I don't think things turned out so bad. I mean, the picture may not have been a complete artistic success ...

CLARK. (*Outraged.*) Not a "complete artistic success"? Not a "complete artistic success"??? (*HE rummages in his bag, pulls out a battered folder of newspaper clippings preserved in plastic, and waves one of them in Hamilton's face.*) No, Hamilton, I don't think you could call a picture *The New York Times* labeled "a trivial, trashy travesty" a *complete* artistic success!

HAMILTON. Well, be that as it may ...

CLARK. Hmph!

(CLARK returns the clipping to the folder, puts the folder back in his bag, and sits back down in the armchair. HAMILTON goes to the bar.)

HAMILTON. Be that as it may, Clark, Vicksburg made a lot of money for *Three Happy Fellas, Inc.* But more important than money, it made a baby. And when the cameras start rolling Monday on *Return* to Vicksburg, I hope you and Derek and I can forget our little artistic differences and make our new baby fly like ... "A silver heron against the crimson Mississippi sun."

CLARK. (*Stares at Hamilton for a moment.*) Did you just make that up?

HAMILTON. Well, I've been kicking it around for a couple of days. Did you like it?

CLARK. It's awful! "A silver heron against the crimson Mississippi sun"? Hamilton, that's ... awful!

HAMILTON. Well, Doodles, that's why you're the writer and I'm the director. (*HAMILTON pours vodka into two glasses and holds one out to Clark.*) Friends?

CLARK. (*Looks at Hamilton for a moment, then takes the glass.*) Well ... colleagues.

(*HAMILTON laughs and slaps Clark on the back. CLARK chokes on his vodka. HAMILTON whips out a handkerchief and dabs at the spilled vodka on Clark's shirt. THEY pay no attention as BARBARA appears at the top of the stairs in a bikini and an open beach jacket.*)

BARBARA. (*Clearing her throat.*) Uh ... mm. Gentlemen. Am I interrupting a "moment"?

HAMILTON. Not at all, darling. Clark and I were just doing a little male bonding.

BARBARA. Well, hooray for the "new man." And there I was just petrified that I'd find you two going at it with clubs and daggers.

HAMILTON. Barbara ...

BARBARA. So, now that we're all friends again ...

CLARK. (*Sharply.*) Colleagues.

BARBARA. (*Descending the stairs.*) Oh, excuse me. Okay, so which one of you "colleagues" wants to join me for a quick plunge into that crystal blue before dinner?

HAMILTON. (*Goes to the computer.*) Barbara. No. I want you to help us go over the changes before Derek gets here.

CLARK. (*Interrupts a bite of Fig Newton.*) Changes? Changes? What changes?

HAMILTON. (*Tossing Clark a Fig Newton.*) Have another Newton, Clark.

CLARK. (*Starting to panic.*) Hamilton, what changes???

BARBARA. Clark ...

CLARK. (*Going to Hamilton at the desk.*) You told me on the phone not one comma. Not one period. Not one dot-dot-dot!

HAMILTON. (*Holding up Clark's manuscript.*) Clark, what you've written, as far as I'm concerned, is perfection.

CLARK. (*Grabs the manuscript and hugs it to his chest.*) Good, because you're not touching it! That's our deal, that's the only reason I've agreed ...

HAMILTON. Clark, it's not me, it's Derek!

CLARK. Derek? Derek??? Who cares about Derek? He's an actor.

HAMILTON. Clark ...

CLARK. A BAD actor.

BARBARA. No, Clark. He's a STAR.

CLARK. Unfortunately.

HAMILTON. *Our* star.

CLARK. Fine. Okay. I can live with that. He is "our" star, and he has a job to do. And that job, that job, is to SAY MY WORDS! I write, you direct, she "publicizes," he ACTS! That's the deal. And if that's not good enough for Derek, then I say we pack the whole thing in and go home!

(CLARK goes to the bar and "calmly" pours himself a drink. HAMILTON looks helplessly at Barbara.)

BARBARA. (*Gently.*) Clark, let's say your screenplay is a basketball ...

CLARK. A BASKETBALL???

BARBARA. (*Going to him.*) No, wait now, hear me out. Let's say it's a basketball, okay? And it's a beautiful basketball, maybe even the most beautiful basketball ever made.

CLARK. (*Disgusted.*) A basketball ...

BARBARA. Okay. Now, it's possible that someone, somewhere, some very sensitive, artistic person, might recognize your basketball for the beautiful piece of art it is, for its perfect roundness, its pleasing color, its wonderfully nubby little skin. And maybe that person could even get your basketball a spot in the Museum of Modern Art, with lots of other esthetically pleasing little balls. We would all be very proud of you, and the few people who actually *noticed* your basketball would say: "Hm, nice basketball." And that would be the end of it. BUT! Suppose you have a friend, a basketball coach, say ... (*SHE gestures toward Hamilton.*) ... who gets your basketball to Michael Jordan. And Michael Jordan takes a look at your basketball and says "Hey, bro, this basketball is swell. I want to PLAY with *this* basketball!" Well. Michael Jordan is going to bounce your basketball around a little bit, right? But even if he scuffs it up a little, hell, even if he paints his initials on it in day-glo orange paint, it's still *your* basketball! Only now, *millions* of people are seeing it! And a little tiny bit of the seven dollars each they're *paying* to see it is going into *your* pocket! And really, Clark, isn't that lots better than leaving that sad, lonely basketball sitting on a little plexiglass stand in the middle of a museum?

CLARK. (*After a beat.*) No! It isn't! I don't want my basketball painted! I don't want it scuffed up! My basketball was happy up on that little stand! Put my basketball back in the museum!

HAMILTON. Nice try, Barbara.

CLARK. I want my basketball back!

HAMILTON. (*Getting up from the desk.*) Okay, Clark, forget the basketball. Forget Michael Jordan. Here's the bottom line. (*HAMILTON lays out the following explanation as though addressing a child.*) You, me, *and Derek* all signed the articles of incorporation for *Three Happy Fellas. Inc.* That means we are all *locked* into this partnership. *But* even though we are all—legally—*equal* partners, it is Derek Coburn's name that sold our little movies to Pegasus Pictures. Not Clark Robinson's, not Hamilton Orr's. So. Derek Coburn can change your script as often as he changes his underwear because on this movie, Derek Coburn has more power than GOD! Now. Those are the facts of life, *partner*, and there's not a damn thing either one of *us* can do to change them.

(There is a moment of silence as CLARK lets the facts of life sink in.)

CLARK. But Derek is so ... so ... shallow! He'll want to play every scene with his shirt off and change all my best lines to "huh."

BARBARA. I know. I feel horrible about it. Especially after I spoke to Bill Put ...

HAMILTON. Shut up, Barbara!

CLARK. Bill Put? Bill Put? You mean William Putnam? You spoke to William Putnam?

HAMILTON. (*Sitting in the chair.*) It's nothing, Clark. It doesn't matter now, anyway.

CLARK. What doesn't matter now? Why did you speak to William Putnam?

(BARBARA is silent.)

CLARK. Barbara, why did you speak to William Putnam??

BARBARA. Oh, Clark, Hamilton didn't want me to tell you. Bill called from London a few weeks ago, very upset. His agent hadn't even *shown* him your screenplay! But when Bill finally got around to reading the copy Hamilton sent to his home, he couldn't put it down.

CLARK. And? And?

HAMILTON. He wanted to play Howard Howard Lawton.

CLARK. What? I ... I thought he only worked with Sir Cecil Harrington.

HAMILTON. No, Mr. Putnam had no qualms about working with me.

BARBARA. But it was too late, Clark. We were already locked into Derek.

CLARK. But that's crazy! William Putnam is a genius!

HAMILTON. Clark ...

CLARK. No! This is insane! We could have had William Putnam and we're stuck with Derek Coburn, because some "executives" like the way he grunts and sweats? I quit! I have to try to keep what little sanity I've got left!

(CLARK runs out of the room, onto the porch, and down the steps. HAMILTON goes to the door and calls after him.)

HAMILTON. I hope you're a fast swimmer. It's seven miles. And when these barracudas eat you alive, it's not a metaphor, it's a meal!

BARBARA. Darling. Easy. You know, a good director is like a puppeteer. And a puppeteer must keep a steady hand.

HAMILTON. (*Goes to her and gives her a light kiss. Then HE moves his hands up her body and rests them on her throat.*) Get him back. And if you have to use your most powerful lure, do wait until after dinner. I've got to get some sleep.

BARBARA. Hamilton, please.

(BARBARA goes out the door to the beach. HAMILTON holds out his hands and spreads his fingers, then raises them one at a time like a puppeteer.)

HAMILTON. "Puppeteer" ... With one little flick ...

(HE begins to laugh softly to himself as he "flicks the fates" of his puppets. BARBARA calls from beyond the porch.)

BARBARA. (*Offstage.*) Hamilton? He'll come back and talk, if you ask nicely and promise not to yell.

HAMILTON. Idiots. (*HE goes to the door and calls out sweetly.*) Clark, sweetheart, please come back and help make the best of the situation.

(HE goes to the bar and waits. BARBARA leads CLARK in by the hand.)

HAMILTON. Barbara, could you give the two of us a few minutes, please? There are some things I'd like to "share" with Clark ... alone.

(BARBARA goes upstairs.)

CLARK. I just ... I ... uh ...

HAMILTON. Please. (*HE pours two drinks and offers one to Clark.*) Look. I know how important your work is to you. And I know Vicksburg put you under for a little while.

CLARK. You don't know the half of it.

HAMILTON. I do, Clark. Barbara told me what happened that night of the screening.

CLARK. She what??

HAMILTON. Clark ....

CLARK. Then you know ...?

HAMILTON. I know *everything*. Clark, I was shocked. It was just a movie ...

CLARK. Don't tell me it was "just a movie"! These are my real-life ancestors I'm writing about, my flesh and blood!

HAMILTON. But *suicide*, Clark.

CLARK. (*Sitting in the chair.*) I know. I know. I've worked it all out now, in the hospital, in therapy. "I am me, I am not my work, I DO my work, but my work is not me." I know. But you can't begin to understand how devastating it was to see my work defiled like that!

HAMILTON. Yes I can! Look, I feel the same way you do about Derek.

CLARK. But you're the one who made him a partner!

HAMILTON. I know, but I had to! Dammit, Clark, you're not the only "artist" in this partnership. But I have to wear two hats. As producer, I *produce*. Word goes out on the street that Pegasus Pictures is hot for Derek Coburn, I sign him up, next thing you know, we've got a table right next to the president of Pegasus at the Polo Lounge. Bottle of champagne here, bottle of champagne there, couple of gals, and we got a three picture deal. Hell, man, it's all done with smoke and mirrors and I'm the master.

CLARK. But my script?

HAMILTON. Sssh ... Sssh ... Sssh. So much for the producer hat. Now the director hat. (*HE downs his drink.*) As the director, from the moment I first read your screenplay, I am constantly forming a vision. Yes, it's inspired by your words and story, but it is *my* vision. And Clark, that vision is the perfect movie, the movie we all hope we'll see every time we settle into our cushy seats, smelling the popcorn and waiting for the lights to go down. But it can't happen unless I get that perfect movie out of my head and onto ten thousand feet of celluloid. So for the past nine weeks, eighteen hours a day, I've been living with a view finder attached to my right eye working out every shot, every angle, every move, all the time Vladimir yelling "impossible, impossible" in my ear, but still hanging on for dear life to *my vision* ...

CLARK. I guess I never really thought ...

HAMILTON. Sssh! Now. Yesterday, I worked out this move, probably the most spectacular dolly shot since Lawrence of Arabia. (*HAMILTON dramatically enacts the following for Clark in great detail, using the entire room and ultimately creating the final "shot" on an imaginary movie screen down center.*) The dawn breaks. (*HE begins to hum the Lawrence of Arabia theme.*) After three generations of torment, Howard Howard Lawton has finally rid the land of the last Howard. He's out on the veranda, silhouetted against the decaying columns of the family plantation home. I don't start too far back. Streaks of sunlight filter through the morning mist. Then, as Howard Howard starts across the great lawn under the big oaks, I shoot through the cedars, moving with him, moving, moving all the time. And as he climbs up the east side of the levee, I'm following his every step, dollying right out over the Mississippi river! And as Howard Howard Lawton reaches the spot where his great great granddaddy died, I'm moving that camera up, up, up that levee ... and when the first birthing blast of sunlight hits his face, I'm on a tight, tight close-up that will be ninety feet high on the giant screen of ...? Of ...?

CLARK. (*Leaps up and screams at the imaginary screen.*) Of DEREK COBURN! No!!

HAMILTON. Yes!!!

(THEY turn and look at each other.)

HAMILTON.	CLARK.
Aaaarrggghhh!	Aaaarrggghhh!

HAMILTON. So you see how I feel??

CLARK. Yes! I hate him! I hate him!

(THEY both scream the following lines at the imaginary screen.)

HAMILTON. Right! I hate him, too! I could kill him!

CLARK. Yes! Yes! Yes!

HAMILTON. Yes! (*Pause.*) Well. That felt good.

CLARK. (*Sheepishly.*) Yes. Yes, it did, actually. It was, um, nice to get that out.

HAMILTON. Right.

CLARK. Hamilton, I, um, I'm sorry. I'm sorry I never took you more seriously. I mean, as an artist, you know, the vision thing, I'm sorry ...

HAMILTON. Forget it. (*HAMILTON goes to bar and refills their glasses.*) But, you know, I wonder, Clark. Could we? Could we really?

CLARK. What?

HAMILTON. Kill someone. Derek. For our art.

CLARK. Well, no. Not really.

HAMILTON. No. I guess not. (*Taking a last look at the imaginary screen.*) Too bad.

CLARK. Yeah. (*CLARK takes his glass and sits on the sofa.*)

HAMILTON. Well, maybe we could add some exceptionally dangerous stunts into the film ....

(THEY laugh.)

CLARK. Right ... Let's have him dive into a school of piranha. It's a shame there aren't any piranhas in the Mississippi.

HAMILTON. (*Sits in the armchair.*) Well, hell, Doodles, you're the writer, why don't you just have him blow his brains out in the opening scene?

CLARK. Right! Blow his brains out ... But we'd have to promise him he'd still get the girl in the end, or he'd never do it. (*HE mimes putting a pistol to his head and speaks à la Derek.)* Go ahead and laugh, baby. You're next. Bam!

HAMILTON. *(Laughing.)* Right, right. Property! Oh, props. There weren't supposed to be real bullets in this gun. Darn it!

CLARK. I love it. I love it!

HAMILTON. But it would never work. The prop man would never go along with us.

CLARK. Why not?

HAMILTON. Murder is a different union.

CLARK. (*Howling with laughter.*) Too bad.

(HAMILTON and CLARK play the following "plotting" lightly and without menace, as though they were simply working the story line for a film.)

HAMILTON. So, forget the prop man. Make it a rehearsal. Informal. Just the three of us going over rewrites. No lights, no cameras, no witnesses.

CLARK. No, no. We'd need witnesses to swear it was an accident.

HAMILTON. Maybe it wouldn't have to look like an accident.

CLARK. What do you mean?

HAMILTON. Maybe we could make it look like a real suicide! Listen to this, Clark, this is great. We call Derek in to rehearse a new scene that just happens to include his character's suicide. Bang, oops, we destroy the script before the coroner gets here ...

CLARK. (*Getting into the spirit of the fantasy.*) And we testify that he showed up here depressed, drunk, and irrational, then suddenly pulled out a gun ... uh-oh, where would he get the gun?

HAMILTON. Hmm.

CLARK. He's got to have a gun!

HAMILTON. (*Looks around the room and spots the governor's antique oak rifle case.*) Governor Bob! (*In a heavy southern accent.*) Bless his heart. (*HAMILTON takes out a 12 gauge double barrel shotgun and holds it up for inspection.*)

CLARK. A shotgun? Uch! Too messy.

HAMILTON. Right. You're right. Pistol? (*HE rummages in the drawer of the gun case and pulls out a .38 caliber revolver.*) Ah! Much better. A .38 caliber. Won't even spoil his profile. (*HE begins to pace the room, acting out the "rehearsal" scenario.*) You know, Derek, the scene's still missing something. I know! Try using this perfectly safe, empty, bullet-free revolver, just to get the feel of it.

CLARK. (*Taking the pistol, à la Derek.*) Hey, man, I dunno, man, lemme see that. Wait a minute, Mr. Big Shot Director. This baby's not empty! Take that! Bang, bang, bang!

(HE gives the pistol back to Hamilton. HAMILTON replaces it in the drawer.)

CLARK. Bad plan, Hamilton. Too risky. Way too risky. Stick to directing.

HAMILTON. All right. You're right. Let's see ... aha! (*HE moves to the case where the two identical revolvers are displayed and reads the commemorative plaque.*) "For Robert 'Skippy' Tubbman—a real straight shooter ..."

CLARK. "Skippy"???

HAMILTON. "Love and *Kisses*, Mamie Eisenhower, Christmas, 1958." (*Laughing, HE removes one of the pistols—Pistol #1—and empties the cylinder, putting the shells in his pocket.*)

CLARK. My God! Governor Bob and *Mamie Eisenhower*? Oooh.

HAMILTON. Clark, look at these two pistols. Can you tell the difference?

CLARK. No.

HAMILTON. Exactly! (*Using his handkerchief, HAMILTON takes the other identical revolver—Pistol #2—from the case and hides it behind his back. Then, holding out Pistol #1, HE addresses Clark as though Clark were Derek.*) Hey, Derek, check out this revolver to make sure it's perfectly safe. Okay?

(CLARK nods. HAMILTON puts Pistol #1 on the coffee table.)

HAMILTON. Okay. Oh, Derek, look at the hooters on that babe! (*HE switches the guns.*) Too late, she's gone. Well, go ahead Derek, try the scene again.

CLARK. Aaaahh ... that's good, it's good ... BUT!

HAMILTON. But what?

CLARK. *(Indicating Pistol #2 on the table.)* He could still check the pistol *again* for bullets before he starts to play the scene.

HAMILTON. Okay, okay, give me a minute. Let's see. Okay! *(HAMILTON picks up Pistol #2 with the handkerchief, and, holding it behind his back again, HE improvises the following scenario with great animation.)* Derek, in this scene you, uh, you're in a rage. Your Uncle Norton is there in that chair, Derek, and he's laughing at you. And you can't bear to hear that laugh ever again. So you whip out your pistol and fire a shot right through Uncle Norton's heart. Bang. *(HE fires Pistol #1 at the chair. The pistol clicks.)* Horrified by your action, you put the pistol on the table ... *(HE puts Pistol #1 on the coffee table.)* ... and rush to the window, seeking an escape. But below you on the grounds, your mother's garden party is in full swing ...

CLARK. Garden party??

HAMILTON. Shut up, I'm on a roll. Your mother's garden party is in full swing, and you realize what a hollow sham your life has become. You scream to the crowd below: "I don't want to live any more!!" *(HAMILTON takes Pistol #2 from behind his back and switches it with Pistol #1 on the table.) Then* you rush back to the table, you pick up the pistol, and WITHOUT EVEN STOPPING TO LOOK AT IT, you put it to your head, pull the trigger, and end your miserable, narcissistic, self-centered, vile existence. Bang. Oops. Oh, Mr. Putnam?

(HAMILTON bows and CLARK applauds.)

CLARK. Great! Great! Bravo! I love it. It's perfect.

HAMILTON. *(Simply.)* Let's do it.

CLARK. What?

BARBARA. *(Appears at the top of the stairs.)* What is going on down here? I thought you two were supposed to be having a serious talk?

HAMILTON. *(Hides the pistols under the sofa cushions.)* We moved on to lighter conversation. It happens.

BARBARA. *(Descending the stairs.)* Well, it was wonderful to hear the two of you laughing together again. I only hope you can keep it up—I just saw the water taxi pulling in. Probably Derek.

CLARK. Oh, no.

HAMILTON. *(Goes to the computer and begins to type.)* Good. Go meet him at the dock, Barbara, but stall him for a few minutes, will you? Clark and I still have a bit more we need to discuss.

BARBARA. All right. But don't expect me to keep him entertained long. I'm afraid I'm just not his type. After all, I'm old enough to drive in most states. *(BARBARA exits out the front door.)*

HAMILTON. *(Typing.)* We'll have to work fast. Let me sketch out the scene.

CLARK. Hamilton, what are you doing? We were just kidding around!

HAMILTON. That's how some of the greatest ideas get started. God was probably kidding around when he invented sex.

CLARK. No, this is crazy! You can't kill somebody just for being a bad actor!

HAMILTON. When they're as bad as Derek, it's justifiable homicide. (*HAMILTON hits some keys on the computer and a page begins to churn out. HE goes to the sofa, raises the cushion, and takes out Pistol #1.*) All right. This is pistol number one. Prop gun. Empty gun. (*HE clicks the trigger a few times and puts Pistol #1 back into its place in the display case. Then, during the following speech, HE takes out his handkerchief and carefully checks the chamber of Pistol #2.*) And this ... this is pistol number two. Fully loaded, just the way Governor Bob left it, perfectly legal protection ... The only prints the coroner will find on this gun are Derek's and Governor Bob's. (*HE replaces Pistol #2 in the display case.*) And since Governor Bob is in Djakarta, *his* alibi is solid. It's a textbook case of suicide.

CLARK. Hamilton, wait!

HAMILTON. No! We can't wait! This is perfect. Our vision, Clark. Think of our vision! Now read this. (*HAMILTON rips the sheet from the printer and holds it out to Clark.*)

CLARK. Hamilton ...

HAMILTON. Read it, dammit!

CLARK. No! I won't read it! I don't want any part of this!

HAMILTON. Dammit, Clark, don't you understand? This is our shot at that perfect movie! We both know it can't happen with Derek, but it *can* happen with Bill Putnam! Think of how you felt just now seeing Derek's face up on that giant screen!

CLARK. But Hamilton, we could go to jail for the rest of our lives! This is murder!

HAMILTON. No, Clark, it's perfect! Derek screams out the window that he's going to kill himself, puts a pistol to his head, and does. We have our movie back in our hands, and with Derek out of the picture, so to speak, Pegasus will jump at the chance to sign William Putnam! Don't you see? It's too perfect. We're *meant* to do this!

CLARK. How can you say that? How can you be serious? We're talking about murder! About taking a human life! And every human life, no matter how shallow it seems on the surface, is sacred! No human being is totally worthless!

(Suddenly the door bursts open and DEREK COBURN stands framed in the doorway. HE is very tan and very loud.)

DEREK. Hey, Ham! Doodles! How ya doin'? (*HE comes in and looks around the room.*) Man, this place is far out. BarBar told me it was out of the way, but dudes! How we gonna stay connected, you know? You got a ... oh, good, right. (*HE goes to the bar and downs a large shot of vodka.*) Oh, man. Yeah. Whew.

(BARBARA enters, loaded down with Derek's bags. During the following, DEREK changes into swim trunks behind the bar.)

DEREK. Yo, BarBar, where's my blue bag? Oh yeah, gimme ... Listen, did you guys take the water taxi? Oh, man, did you see the ta-tas on that babe? Must be Daddy's boat, huh? I mean still in high school, probably, but out to here, man, out to here, and *ripe*? Mmm, mmm, mmm! Sorry BarBar, but they love me, what can I say? Shoot me.

(CLARK and HAMILTON exchange a look.)

DEREK. Listen, I told her there might be something for her in the picture, you know? I mean, toss her a bone, what the hell, right? Yeah, I'd like to be tossing her a bone right now, yeah ... Joke, BarBar, come on! I mean, man, I wanna keep that one around a while. Dumb as a post, but out-to-here, man! I thought maybe she could play like the chick who's what's-his-name's first lay or whatever, like the one who was supposed to be your grandmother or something, Clark, like in real life? Whatever ... (*HE empties the vodka bottle into his glass.*) Hey, you got any more of this? No, wait a minute, never mind. *(HE takes a vial of coke from his bag.)* Never mix never worry, right? Has it been five minutes? Joke! (*HE snorts the coke.*) Listen, I gotta get back before she swims upstream to spawn, man. It's been real. If I'm not back by dawn, send out the punetang patrol. Sorry, BarBar. Later, dudes.

(DEREK sweeps out the front door. There is silence for a moment, then CLARK rushes to the door and calls after him.)

CLARK. Derek! Come back! We have to rehearse a whole new ending!

BARBARA. What? What new ending? Does Vladimir know about this?

CLARK. Derek!!

HAMILTON. (*Escorting her to the door.*) Never mind, Barbara, why don't you go ahead and have that swim? This won't take long. Then we'll all send over to the mainland for some dinner, and talk about that *Premiere* spread, and talk shows ... anything your little publicity heart desires, okay?

BARBARA. Oh, all right.

HAMILTON. Good girl.

CLARK. DEREK!!!!

BARBARA. Save your lungs, Clark. I'll send him back. If I can tear him away from Lolita. Maybe we should have *her* arrested for contributing to the delinquency of an imbecile.

(And SHE is gone. CLARK closes the door behind her and turns to Hamilton.)

CLARK. Okay. Okay. Good. Good. What do we do first? Where's the scene?

HAMILTON. Clark, calm down. We have to act perfectly natural. Convince him we're just working out an artistic choice you made for the good of the picture.

CLARK. Artistic choice for the good of the picture, right. And it is! It is, Hamilton, isn't it?

HAMILTON. Yes, Clark, it is. Definitely. Now. The only tricky part will be switching the pistols. Um ... Leave that to me.

CLARK. (*Searching frantically for the scene.*) Right. Okay. So when he gets here, we show him the scene ... Oh, Jesus, where's the scene?

HAMILTON. (*Hands him the scene.*) Clark! It's right here! Relax! Now sit down. Gather your power. Think of your ancestors.

CLARK. Right. Okay. Right.

(*CLARK sits in the armchair. A beat, then DEREK enters. CLARK leaps up.*)

DEREK. Dudes, dudes, what's happening? I thought we were cool, all systems go, green light city. So what's with this new scene crap? Dudes, if it ain't broke, don't fix it, you know?

HAMILTON. Clark just had a brilliant idea, Derek, and we, ah, we wanted to get your input. It won't take long, and then you can get right back to your little friend on the dock.

DEREK. (*Goes to his bag, rummages through clothes, and during the following, pulls a designer jump suit on over his swim trunks.*) Oh, forget it, man, bitch took off, didn't wait. Must've got cold feet. Big tits, cold feet, is that what they say?

(*CLARK and HAMILTON stare at him.*)

DEREK. What?

HAMILTON. Something like that. Anyway, Clark, why don't you tell Derek what we've been kicking around?

(*HAMILTON goes to the door and locks it.*)

CLARK. Right. Yes. Well. Ah, Derek, we think, that is, we've been, uh, kicking around the possibility of having your character, Howard ...

DEREK. Yeah, right, Howard Howard Lawton, my main man ...

CLARK. Yes. Well, we think perhaps Howard should, um, should take his own life in the final scene of the film.

(Pause.)

HAMILTON. That he should perhaps shoot himself in the head.

CLARK. With a pistol.

HAMILTON. In the head.

CLARK. In the final scene.

HAMILTON. Yes.

(Pause.)

DEREK. What?

CLARK. That Howard Howard should take ...

DEREK. Yeah, yeah, yeah, I heard you, man, but what the hell are you talking about?

CLARK. Well, it's uh, it's very simple, it actually follows from the character's pain and struggle ...

DEREK. Hey, I don't give a damn about the character's pain and struggle. I just know I don't want people walking out of the damn theater with their last image being *me* splattered all over the screen!

HAMILTON. It wouldn't ... necessarily have to be like that. We could, ah, we could do a montage of the good times, you know, all your best moments, over the closing credits.

DEREK. No way, man. The only people who stay for the credits are the teenagers who sweep up the popcorn. Forget it, dudes.

CLARK. Derek! Just listen! Some of the greatest characters in literature have killed themselves. Think of Ibsen. Think of Shakespeare, for God's sake.

DEREK. Shakespeare killed himself?

CLARK. No, Derek, Shakespeare's characters!

DEREK. Oh.

HAMILTON. Right. Derek, Mel Gibson got to play Hamlet because Franco Zeffirelli liked the way he *contemplated* suicide in Lethal Weapon. True story. Hell, man, if you *go through with it,* you'll be playing King Lear!

DEREK. Yeah?? Now, wait a minute, wait a minute, which one was he? Not the one with the hump ...

(CLARK groans.)

HAMILTON. No, Derek, he was the sexy one.

DEREK. Yeah? All right, man! But still ...

HAMILTON. Derek, let's forget about Shakespeare. I want to talk about you.

DEREK. Yeah, great, okay, let's do that.

(DEREK sits on the sofa. HAMILTON begins pacing.)

HAMILTON. I've been thinking about you a lot lately, Derek, about your work, I mean, and I can't help feeling something ... well, something is missing. As ...

memorable ... as your portrayal of Howard Howard was in Vicksburg I, somehow it lacked a certain, how shall I say it? A ... resonance that you so abundantly possess in person ...

CLARK. (*Under his breath.*) Jesus.

HAMILTON. And I really think it was because you were just too darn good for the material.

CLARK. What??

HAMILTON. Clark! Now, I've discussed this with Clark, and *he agrees.* And this latest rewrite is his attempt to enrich the script to accommodate the full breadth of your talent. Right, Clark?

CLARK. (*Going to Derek.*) Ah, yes. Yes. You see, Derek, by, um, by making Howard Howard a character whose principles run so deep that their violation would lead him to take his own life, we, um, create a persona on screen that ... that ...

HAMILTON. That gives you room to explore the vastness of your talent, Derek, to fill the screen with something besides charm and boyish good looks.

CLARK. Right.

DEREK. What's wrong with charm and boyish good looks?

HAMILTON. Nothing! Nothing at all, they're terrific assets, wonderful qualities. But great stars are made of more than that. And, Derek, you deserve to be a great star.

DEREK. Yeah?

HAMILTON. Yes! I'm talking about the kind of star who gets his picture on the cover of *People* magazine *and* the Arts and Leisure section of the *Sunday New York Times* in the *same week*, Derek! And if we can do what I have in mind with this movie, come next April ... I'm thinking of a little gold statue whose name begins with "O."

DEREK. (*Stares blankly at Hamilton for a moment.*) How many letters?

HAMILTON. Oscar, Derek! I'm talking Academy Award!

DEREK. Aw, come on, man!

HAMILTON. Yes! And it's all right here!

(HAMILTON grabs the scene from Clark. In his nervousness, CLARK has crumpled the scene into a small ball.)

HAMILTON. Derek, if you take this scene into your soul, if you can breathe life into it the way I know you can, it will color your whole performance, from the very first frame of the film, and make it the performance that puts Derek Coburn over the top!

DEREK. (*Jumping up and grabbing the scene.*) Well, hey, okay dude, let's do it!

HAMILTON. Great!

CLARK. (*Beginning to pace nervously.*) Oh, God ...

HAMILTON. Now...

DEREK. Wait a minute, wait a minute, let me read it.

HAMILTON. (*Grabbing the scene back from Derek.*) That's okay, Derek, let me just run it by you. If you like it, we can work on the lines later.

CLARK. Oh, God ...

HAMILTON. Now. Let's put your Uncle Norton Howard in that chair ... Clark, be Uncle Norton, will you?

CLARK. What?

HAMILTON. Sit in for Uncle Norton. Derek needs someone to relate to.

CLARK. (*Sitting in the chair.*) Oh. Yes. I see. All right. Here?

HAMILTON. Fine. Now, Derek, you've had your big confrontation with Uncle Norton, and it's been fruitless. In fact, he's laughed in your face. Laugh at Derek, Clark.

(CLARK laughs weakly.)

HAMILTON. Right. It'll be stronger when we have the actor, but you get the idea. So.

DEREK. What do I do when ...

HAMILTON. Sssh! Just absorb it for now. Breathe it in. All right? Good. Now. That laugh touches something in you, Derek. It ridicules your heritage, your whole existence. So you whip out your revolver, which you've been forced to carry everywhere for your own protection, and you wipe out that laugh with a bullet through Uncle Norton's heart.

(DEREK suddenly draws and fires an imaginary pistol at Clark.)

DEREK. Bang! Bang, bang, bang!

CLARK. (*Diving behind chair.*) Jesus Christ!

HAMILTON. Good, Derek! Very good! That's the feeling! But just one shot. A single, sharp statement. All right?

DEREK. Yeah, okay, right, one shot. Got it. (*Firing at Clark again.*) BANG!

CLARK. Hey!

HAMILTON. Good! Get up, Clark. Now, think of what you've done, Derek. You've taken a life, the life of a member of your family. It's the ultimate corruption, and it puts you over the edge. You drop the revolver on the table and rush to the window, you have to breathe! But on the great lawn below is a party. Very stuffy, everything you hate, it's uh, it's your little niece's coming out party ...

DEREK. (*Interrupting.*) My little niece is gay?

CLARK. Oh my God ...

HAMILTON. No, Derek! Debutantes! It's just a fancy party, very pretentious, very artificial. It's a betrayal of your ideals! So you scream out your pain ...

(DEREK lets out a mighty scream; HAMILTON and CLARK jump.)

HAMILTON. Ah ... good! Then you yell to them all that you don't want to live any more, and in a rage, you rush back to the table, snatch up your revolver and put it to your temple. Then you say your final line ... Derek, try that line ...

DEREK. (*Checking the script.*) Uh, let's see, um ... "I have become too poisoned to live."

HAMILTON. Beautiful! Then you pull the trigger, and that's it! (*HE turns to an imaginary TV camera.*) "May I have the envelope, please?"

DEREK. You really think so?

HAMILTON. No question. No question! Want to put it on its feet?

DEREK. Yeah, sure, what the hell.

(DEREK goes upstage and begins a noisy loosening up ritual. CLARK pulls HAMILTON aside.)

CLARK. Hamilton, I can't do this. I can't go through with this.

HAMILTON. You don't have to do anything, Clark. The movie's already started. You're not responsible for how it ends.

CLARK. But ...

DEREK. (*Comes back downstage to Hamilton and Clark, ready to play the scene.*) Okay! Ready to roll.

HAMILTON. All right, Derek! Now ... Dammit, I wish we had some props here. It looks so silly for him to point his finger and say bang, I can't get the full picture ... I know! Let's borrow one of the governor's pistols. (*HE goes to the pistol case and removes Pistol #1.*) Check this to make sure it's empty, Derek, then play with it a little just to get the feel of it, okay?

DEREK. Hey, man, this is cool. (*DEREK quickly checks the chamber of the revolver, then springs into a cop movie pose and speaks à la Eastwood.*) Go ahead. Make my day. (*HE wheels on Clark and Hamilton.*) Boom! Boom! Boom!

CLARK. Oh God, oh Jesus ...

HAMILTON. Right, Derek, very good, but now let's come back to Mississippi, shall we? That pistol *is* empty, right?

DEREK. Yeah, sure, no problem.

HAMILTON. All right, then, let's go to work. Now, Clark, would you sit in for Uncle Norton again, please?

CLARK. No.

(HAMILTON gives him a look.)

CLARK. No. I don't want to.
HAMILTON. Clark!
CLARK. No!
DEREK. Aw, come on, man!
CLARK. NOO!!!

HAMILTON. (*Glaring at Clark.*) Well, you know, perhaps he's right, Derek, he does need to see this from the camera's POV, so just play the chair as though it were Uncle Norton, all right? Any problem with that?

DEREK. Hell no, no problem. I don't need anybody else to act with. You know me.

HAMILTON. Right. I forgot. Fine. So, ready? Let's take it from the top. Watch carefully, Clark.

(CLARK gives Hamilton a look. DEREK rolls his head, takes a couple of breaths, sets his jaw, and strikes an "acting" pose.)

DEREK. (*Through clenched teeth.*) Ready.

HAMILTON. And ... action! All right, see the chair, Derek, see Uncle Norton, he's smiling, he's smiling, see the smile, good, he's starting to laugh, he's laughing at *you* Derek, feel the laugh, feel it! What do you want to do? Do it! Do it, Derek!

DEREK. (*Whipping out the pistol.*) You son of a bitch! Take that! (*DEREK fires at the empty chair; the pistol clicks.*)

HAMILTON. Good, Derek, good improvisation! Did you get that line down, Clark? Good.

DEREK. Thanks.

HAMILTON. No! Don't break it! Don't lose it! Now, look at the body, Derek. Look at the pistol. Feel bad. Feel really bad, Derek ...

(DEREK begins to groan.)

HAMILTON. Good! Perfect! Now, hate that gun, Derek. Hate it! Do you hate it?

(DEREK nods.)

HAMILTON. Good! Put it down on the table.

(DEREK puts the pistol down on the coffee table.)

HAMILTON. Great! Now, you need to breathe, you're suffocating, you're drowning, where can you get air? Look for air, Derek ...

(DEREK begins searching frantically around the room for air, picks up one of the cardboard boxes and looks inside.)

HAMILTON. The window! Go for the window, Derek!

(DEREK runs to the window. HAMILTON takes out his handkerchief, removes Pistol #2 from the pistol case, and, during the following, switches it with Pistol #1 on the coffee table.)

HAMILTON. There's the party down there, Derek, it's everything you hate, and it makes you scream. Tell them how you feel, scream, say it!

DEREK. (*After a mighty scream.*) I don't want to live any more!

(DEREK races back to the table and grabs the revolver. HE puts it to his head. CLARK crouches beside the desk.)

HAMILTON. (*In a fierce whisper.*) Now, say your final line, Derek. Say it.

DEREK. I have become too poisoned to live.

(DEREK's hand shakes. CLARK buries his face in his hands. HAMILTON hides behind the sofa. A beat. DEREK pulls the trigger. The pistol clicks. *DEREK falls to the floor.*

There is stunned silence for a moment. CLARK and HAMILTON slowly rise and peer down at Derek.)

DEREK. (*Popping up.*) Well?

HAMILTON.	CLARK.
Aaahhh!!!	Aaahhh!!!

DEREK. How was I?

(DEREK points the pistol at HAMILTON and CLARK, who raise their hands in the air.)

HAMILTON. How were you? How were you? You were ... brilliant! Yes! It, uh, it was very moving, very ... uh, yes, hm, I need a drink! (*HE picks up the empty vodka bottle.*) Derek, we're going to need more than this, a lot more than this, would you, uh, go to the kitchen and get another bottle from the cabinet, please? Or some ice? Or something, in the kitchen ...

DEREK. Yeah, sure.

(DEREK puts the pistol down on the desk and exits to the kitchen. HAMILTON and CLARK watch him until he disappears into the kitchen, then both race to the pistol.)

CLARK. What happened? What the hell happened??

HAMILTON. I don't know. I don't know!

(Using his handkerchief, HAMILTON grabs the pistol and flips open the cylinder. HE takes out the bullet. CLARK drops to his knees.)

CLARK. It's a sign! We can't do this! Thank you, lord. It's a sign!

HAMILTON. (*Holds up the bullet.*) It's not a sign, Clark, it's a dud.

CLARK. A ... dud?

HAMILTON. (*Goes to the drawer of the oak gun case and takes out a new box of ammunition.*) Yes! A dud. Damned pistol probably hasn't been fired since 1958. Now, get hold of yourself. I'll reload with new ammunition and we'll run the scene again!

(There is a loud POUNDING on the front door.)

BARBARA. (*Calling from porch.*) Hamilton. Hamilton!

HAMILTON. (*Looking toward the door, surprised.*) Damn!

BARBARA. (*POUNDING.*) Hamilton, what's wrong? Why was Derek screaming?

(DEREK pops back in from the kitchen, holding a jar of pickled plums. HAMILTON hides the pistol and ammunition behind his back.)

DEREK. I can't find vodka. Is this drinkable?

HAMILTON. Derek! Go back! Keep looking!

BARBARA. (*Keeps POUNDING.*) Hamilton! Let me in.

HAMILTON. Barbara! Go away! We don't need you yet!

DEREK. But it's a Safeway in there, man, I mean shelves and jars and all these ugly ...

HAMILTON. Just go back, dammit, and find anything alcoholic!

DEREK. Okay, dude. Chill. Jeez.

(DEREK disappears back into the kitchen. BARBARA keeps POUNDING.)

BARBARA. Hamilton!!!

HAMILTON. Damn! Damn!

CLARK. (*Rushes to Hamilton and takes the handkerchief and pistol.*) Here. Give it to me. I can load it! Oh, God, what am I doing?

(CLARK grabs the box of ammunition from Hamilton; it slips from his hand; bullets scatter across the floor.)

HAMILTON. Idiot!!

CLARK. Go! Go! I've got it. I'm okay! I'm okay.

BARBARA. (*Still POUNDING.*) Hamilton! Darling!

HAMILTON. (*Flustered.*) All right, you load it. But I'll make the switch!

(*CLARK scoops up bullets and crawls under the desk to reload the pistol. HAMILTON goes to the door and unlocks it. BARBARA bursts in.*)

BARBARA. Are you all right? I heard screaming.

HAMILTON. (*Blocking her from entering room.*) Yes, darling, everything's fine, we don't need you yet. Go back to your swim.

BARBARA. I don't want to go back to my swim!

(*CLARK emerges from under the desk just as DEREK enters with a half gallon bottle of bourbon.*)

DEREK. Still couldn't find vodka, but there's a whole case of this stuff under the sink.

BARBARA. Derek?

HAMILTON. Yes, fine, Derek. Now, Barbara, just lie in the sun for awhile, dammit, and come back later! (*HAMILTON pushes her out the door and locks it behind her.*)

BARBARA. Hamilton!?

(*And she is gone. HAMILTON looks at Clark, CLARK holds up the pistol behind Derek's back, gives Hamilton the "okay" sign that the pistol is loaded, and carefully sets it on the desk where Derek left it. HAMILTON takes the bottle of bourbon from Derek and pours a large drink.)*

DEREK. So. What'd you think?

HAMILTON. I guess it'll have to do. (*Taking a drink.*) Aaahhhhh.

DEREK. No, Ham, the scene! What did you think of the scene?

HAMILTON. Oh. The scene. Yes.

DEREK. I liked it. I thought I was right on.

HAMILTON. Yes, Derek, so did I, I liked it very much. But Clark has some ... reservations.

DEREK. Reservations are for Indians, man ...

HAMILTON. No, Derek, Clark made some very good points while you were in the kitchen, and I'd like to run the scene one more time *from the top* with his adjustments. We want it perfect for Oscar night, don't we? Go ahead, Clark. Share your feelings.

(During the following, while CLARK keeps Derek distracted, HAMILTON moves to the desk/display case area and, using the handkerchief, switches the pistols for the top of the scene.)

CLARK. Ah. Well. All right. The, um, the reaction to Uncle Norton was very close, very much like what I had in mind, the laughing, the groaning, very good, very good indeed.

DEREK. Like, hey ... the camera should have been rolling. So what's the problem?

(HAMILTON gives Clark the "okay" sign that the pistols have been switched for the top of the scene.)

CLARK. Well, it isn't necessarily a problem, per se, but the colors were slightly, um, muted ... I mean, the nuances ...

DEREK. I don't get it.

(Suddenly BARBARA KNOCKS on the door again.)

BARBARA. Hamilton, dammit, let me in!

HAMILTON. Barbara, just wait!

BARBARA. No! I'm turning B-L-U-E out here. (*BARBARA keeps KNOCKING.*)

DEREK. This is a zoo, man. She's banging, he's talking colors and reservations, I can't work like this. I'm outta here, dudes.

HAMILTON. (*Takes DEREK by the shoulders and sits him in the armchair.*) Derek, sit down. Shut up and listen to the writer. Show him what you want, Clark.

CLARK. What?

BARBARA. (*Keeps KNOCKING.*) Hamilton! Hamilton!

HAMILTON. (*Heads for the door. Indicating the pistol on the desk.*) Come on, Clark, *show* him what you want! I'll get rid of Barbara, and we'll run the scene again! You're Howard Howard, Derek is Uncle Norton, just show him!

CLARK. But ...

BARBARA. Hamilton!

HAMILTON. Dammit Clark! I need a little help here!

DEREK. Hey, Ham, chill.

CLARK. (*Taking the pistol.*) All right! I'm doing it! I'm doing it! I'm showing him!

(HAMILTON opens the door for Barbara as CLARK begins to demonstrate the scene for Derek.)

CLARK. Well. Let's see. Uh ... (*Gesturing broadly with the pistol.*) Argue, argue, argue, then you laugh, you laugh, it makes me very angry, so I pull out my pistol and...

(Suddenly the gun in Clark's hand goes off with a loud BANG, firing a bullet into Derek's chest. The impact of the shot sends the ARMCHAIR toppling over backward. BARBARA screams. The chair crashes into the piano and honky tonk piano MUSIC again fills the room. CLARK stares in horror at the smoking revolver in his hand, then at Hamilton and Barbara in the doorway.

BARBARA rushes past Clark to Derek. HAMILTON goes to the piano and shuts it off. BARBARA kneels beside Derek, feels for his pulse, then turns back to Clark and Hamilton in horror, her hands covered with blood.)

BARBARA. He's dead.

(CLARK faints. The LIGHTS fade.)

END OF ACT I

ACT II

Scene 1

Thirty minutes later.

AT RISE: CLARK lies on the sofa covered with a large Porky Pig beach blanket, trembling and incoherent. BARBARA sits beside him and strokes his hair. HAMILTON paces. An outline of Derek's body has been taped out on the carpet.

THE SHERIFF is at the door, calling offstage.

SHERIFF. Easy, boys, easy now, you're transporting the corpus delicti, not loading feed! Show some respect, here. (*HE turns back to the room.*) I'm sorry, folks ...

(There is a loud CRASH offstage.)

SHERIFF. Watch it, watch it! You drop that damn stiff on Skippy's azaleas and there'll be hell to pay, I can guarantee you, *hell to pay*!! (*HE turns back to the room.*) I'd best make sure those ignoramuses get the movie star's carcass onto the water taxi before they spill him into the Gulf of Mexico and the boy washes up in Aruba. But when I get back, this one here ... *(Indicating Clark.)* ... better be ready to do some serious talking.

(The SHERIFF exits. BARBARA takes Clark's hand.)

BARBARA. Clark? Clark, sweetheart? Come on, now, you have to snap out of it.

CLARK. I didn't know ... I didn't mean to kill him, I ... the gun, oh, my God, he's dead ...

BARBARA. Sssh, sssh, Clark, sit up. Sit up, now. Do you want a drink?

CLARK. No! NO! No drinking! Ever again! NO!

(BARBARA looks to Hamilton, helpless.)

HAMILTON. Take a break, Barbara. Clark, sit up.

CLARK. (*Pulls the blanket over his head.*) NO! I won't listen to you! Ever again!

HAMILTON. Barbara, out! Clark, up! Now! (*HAMILTON goes to the door, looks out, and locks it.*)

BARBARA. Hamilton, don't talk to me like ...

HAMILTON. OUT!!

(BARBARA glares at him for a moment, then turns and exits up the stairs. HAMILTON goes to Clark and hauls him to a sitting position on the sofa.)

CLARK. Hamilton, stop it, what are you doing?

HAMILTON. (*With great urgency.*) Now you listen to me. We don't have much time.

CLARK (*Staring at the blood-stained carpet.*) The gun ... it was empty ... it fired ... how...?

HAMILTON. Shut up. It doesn't matter now. There's only one story that's going to fly here, and you're going to tell it.

CLARK. But ...

HAMILTON. (*Interrupting him.*) This was an *accident*, a *rehearsal accident*, pure and simple. Have you got that? We wrote a new scene. Derek wanted to try it out. The "empty" pistol went off. He's dead. You went into shock. The End.

CLARK. But I *hated* him, and *I pulled the trigger!* How that must look to the police ...

HAMILTON. Clark, this rube Sheriff doesn't know how you felt about Derek! As far as he knows, Derek was the goose about to lay big golden eggs for us all. So why would you want to kill him? No motive, no case.

CLARK. But I *shot* him! Hamilton, I'm a murderer, a cold blooded murderer! What have you done to me?

HAMILTON. Clark! Cold blooded murderers don't faint at the sight of blood. And believe me, you were out. It was all I could do to haul you onto the sofa when Barbara went down to call the sheriff.

CLARK. Oh, my God, Barbara. Does Barbara know ...

HAMILTON. Barbara knows nothing. That story is exactly what I told her while you were passed out, and it's exactly what she told the sheriff on the phone. Barbara's the perfect witness.

CLARK. Oh, Hamilton, I'm so confused, I ... Maybe I should just tell the truth ...

HAMILTON. NO! Listen, Clark, basically nothing has changed. We wanted Derek gone ... (*Indicates Derek's taped out body shape on the floor.*) Derek is *gone*. Right?

CLARK. Right ... but ...

HAMILTON. *But* you have to be strong.

CLARK. Strong?

HAMILTON. Yes! You have to convince the sheriff you want to cooperate fully with the police. Then you have to tell your story as if it were the absolute truth, no whining, no shifty eyes, no stumbling over the details. Because if the good sheriff starts sniffing out the *real* story... well, the death penalty is still very much alive and well in this state, and ...

(There is a KNOCK on the door. CLARK jumps.)

CLARK. All right, you're right. I'll try.

HAMILTON. Good man. I know you can do it, Clark.

CLARK. I think I can.

HAMILTON. I know you can. And I'll be behind you all the way.

(More KNOCKING. HAMILTON heads for the door.)

CLARK. Hamilton?

HAMILTON. What?

CLARK. Thank you. Thank you, Hamilton.

HAMILTON. Chin up, Clark. We'll get through this together. Just remember, cooperating fully with the police. And strong! Gather your power.

(CLARK covers his head with the blanket, then puts his head between his knees and breathes deeply and noisily. HAMILTON opens the door to the sheriff.)

SHERIFF. (*Entering.*) What'd you lock the door for? It's a little late to keep out Mr. Trouble, isn't it?

HAMILTON. Yes, of course, we're just a little jumpy, I guess. Sorry.

SHERIFF. What the hell is he doing?

HAMILTON. He was still a little dizzy. He's just getting his bearings.

SHERIFF. Is he ready to talk?

CLARK. (*His head still between his knees.*) Yes. Just a minute.

SHERIFF. What'd he say?

HAMILTON. He said yes. He's ready to talk.

SHERIFF. Well, good. Is he ready to sit up? Or should I hunker down there on the carpet to listen?

HAMILTON. No, no. He'll sit up. Clark!

(The SHERIFF examines the carpet where the outline of Derek's body has been taped out.)

SHERIFF. Damn! It's going to be hell getting these stains out of Skippy's rug. Murder's a messy business, isn't it?

HAMILTON. Clark! Up! Now! Barbara, come down!

CLARK. (*Sitting up.*) Okay. Yes. I'm ready.

SHERIFF. Well, good morning. Hate like hell to disturb your nap, but since you were apparently the one who did the shooting, I sort of thought you might be useful to my investigation of the killing. It's a theory that's worked for me in the past.

CLARK. Are ... are you going to arrest me?

SHERIFF. Well, I might. (*HE pauses and looks at everyone.)* And then again I might not, depends. If you want me to, I can, and I can tell you all about your rights, and I can get Buck to open up the jail for you, and you can wait there for a few days while your fancy Hollywood lawyers try to work something with Judge Melvin to get you out on bail sometime *fairly* soon ... Or we can sit right here for a few minutes and open a jar of Skippy's good pickles and have a nice little informal chat that won't hold up in court, but will go a hell of long way toward making sure I get back to my garden by dawn. Which would you rather?

(BARBARA has appeared at the top of the stairs. SHE rushes down to Clark.)

BARBARA. Clark, you don't have to say anything! Not if you don't want to.

SHERIFF. *(Heaves a sigh and starts for the door.)* Well, now, you know, the lady's right, she's exactly right, so if you'll just sit tight for a minute, I'll go down to the dock and call Buck ... Uh, let's see. You have the right to remain silent ....

CLARK. No! Stop! *(CLARK jumps up and goes to the sheriff.)*

SHERIFF. Anything you say can *and will* be used against you in a court of law ...

CLARK. Shhh! Shhh! Don't do that! I want to talk. I have nothing to hide. Nothing at all. I want to cooperate fully with the police.

BARBARA. Clark, are you sure? Don't let him intimidate you, Doodles. We'll get you the best lawyer in Beverly Hills.

HAMILTON. Barbara, he said he wants to talk.

(Pause. CLARK looks to Hamilton.)

SHERIFF. *(To Clark.)* Up to you ... Doodles.

CLARK. I'll talk. *(CLARK sits on the sofa.)*

SHERIFF. Well, good. Now is that okay with everybody? Or do we want to all sit here and chat for a little bit longer about whether or not he should talk?

CLARK. No. I want to talk. I want to cooperate fully with the police.

SHERIFF. (*Looks to Barbara.*) Okay?

BARBARA. (*Huffily.*) Fine.

(BARBARA sits. The SHERIFF gestures broadly for Clark to begin.)

CLARK. Okay. Let's see. Um. I really don't know where to start.

SHERIFF. Well, why don't you "take it from the top." Isn't that what you people say?

CLARK. Ah. Yes. All right. Well, as you may know, I'm a writer. A serious writer. At least, I was. But ...

SHERIFF. Wup! Hold it. Excuse me. Forgot the pickles.

HAMILTON. What???

SHERIFF. Pickles. I promised him pickles instead of jail if he decided to talk, remember? (*To Hamilton.*) Would you mind checking in Skippy's pantry for me?

HAMILTON. Me?

SHERIFF. Yessir, should be on the top shelf. 'Bout two dozen jars of the best green tomato pickles you ever tasted.

HAMILTON. You want ME to get PICKLES?

SHERIFF. Yessir, best pickles you ever had in your life! Top shelf. Can't miss 'em.

(HAMILTON glares at the sheriff for a moment. The SHERIFF, all smiles, nods toward the kitchen. HAMILTON turns and huffily heads for the kitchen. The SHERIFF watches until he is out of sight.)

SHERIFF. He *is* awful full of himself, isn't he?

BARBARA. Is this pickle ceremony really necessary? Why don't you just get on with it?

SHERIFF. Tell you the truth, I'm sort of starting to enjoy myself. But you're right. No need to let this drag on all night.

HAMILTON. (*Returns with pickle jar.*) Would you like me to "fetch" some forks?

SHERIFF. Oh, hell no. These are finger pickles. (*HE opens the jar and holds it under Hamilton's nose.*) Smell that. Heaven, heaven, heaven, save a place for me.

(HAMILTON recoils from the smell.)

CLARK. You ... you said green tomatoes?

SHERIFF. That's right, new green tomatoes, have to put 'em up way before anything else is ready, but it is sure worth the trouble. Here.

CLARK. (*Takes a pickle.*) My grandmother used to make green tomato pickles. Oh, God, it smells just like her kitchen in Wiggins.

SHERIFF. (*Suspiciously.*) Your people come from Wiggins?

CLARK. On my mother's side.

SHERIFF. What's your grandmama's name?

CLARK. Um ... Alberta Mumford.

SHERIFF. (*Slaps his knee.*) Ha! *Bertie* Mumford?

CLARK. You knew her?

SHERIFF. Hell, everybody knew Bertie Mumford! Shoot, we could be cousins!

CLARK. Um, well, could be ...

SHERIFF. Well I'll be damned. How the hell did you wind up with this Hollywood bunch?

CLARK. Oh ...

SHERIFF. And what in the world possessed you to murder that boy with the suntan?

BARBARA. This is ludicrous!

HAMILTON. Sheriff! I thought you were going to take it from the top.

SHERIFF. Right. Right. Absolutely right. 'Scuse me. You city folks don't miss a beat, do you? (*The SHERIFF takes out a small notebook and pencil. HE will take occasional notes during the rest of the scene.*) All right. Let's see, now, "the top" ... uh, I believe you were about to tell me what a serious writer you were before you hooked up with these movie people, isn't that right? Go ahead.

CLARK. Well ...

SHERIFF. But I would like to talk some more about your grandmama's pickles sometime.

CLARK. Sure. Okay.

SHERIFF. Go ahead.

CLARK. Um ... Well. This is my second project with Hamilton. And with Barbara. And it was going to be our second project with Derek.

SHERIFF. Derek is the boy you shot?

CLARK. (*Carefully.*) Well, not exactly. I didn't shoot him. He was killed when the gun I was pointing at him went off.

SHERIFF. Uh huh. We'll talk that one through later on. Your second ... "project"?

CLARK. Yes.

SHERIFF. (*Suspiciously.*) So you'd worked with these folks before?

CLARK. Um ... Yes.

SHERIFF. And...?

CLARK. What...?

SHERIFF. (*Exasperated.*) How'd everybody get along?

CLARK. Oh! Well. I, um, I wasn't that happy with our first film, actually. *Vicksburg*? It made a lot of money, but I never really liked it. Did you see it? *Vicksburg*?

SHERIFF. Nope. Why didn't you like it?

CLARK. Because they violated it! They took what I wrote and destroyed it!

SHERIFF. Who did?

CLARK. Derek and Hamilton! They ...

(HAMILTON has a coughing fit. CLARK leaps up and goes to Hamilton.)

CLARK. But that's okay! I mean, we stayed friends and everything! It was just a few little artistic differences, that's all. No problem. Really.

SHERIFF. Uh huh. Well, I'm glad you could work everything out so nice.

CLARK. Oh, yes. So. We were all ready to start this new film ...

SHERIFF. (*Ominously.*) All right, hold it right there! Let's get something straight, here.

(CLARK, HAMILTON, and BARBARA freeze.)

CLARK. Yes?

SHERIFF. You keep talking about this "film." Now, is that the same as a movie? I mean, I say I put film in my Kodak, and go over to the mall to see a movie. Am I saying it wrong?

(Pause.)

CLARK. No, no, you're right, same thing, movie, film, same thing.

SHERIFF. All right. Thanks for clearing that up. Appreciate it. Always wanted to ask somebody about that.

CLARK. Sure.

SHERIFF. Go ahead.

CLARK. Oh. Okay. Where was I? Um. Right. The new, uh, movie. So. We were scheduled to start shooting—oh no, no, no! I mean, to start *filming* next week, but I hadn't really talked to Derek or Hamilton since the first movie, so the governor—a wonderful man, so I'm told—

SHERIFF. Yes he is.

CLARK. Well, he offered Hamilton his, uh, vacation home here so we could, you know, kind of settle in and talk about the screenplay. So Hamilton got here a few days early, but Barbara and I came just this afternoon, and then Derek showed up, and Hamilton and I had worked out this new scene that we wanted Derek to ...

SHERIFF. When?

CLARK. When what?

SHERIFF. When did you two "work out" a new scene? You said you just got here. Doesn't that "creative" stuff take some time?

CLARK. Well ... uh ... sometimes yes, sometimes, no. This was sort of ... spontaneous. (*Pause.*) Sort of a spur of the moment kind of thing. (*Pause.*) Sort of like automatic writing.

(Pause.)

SHERIFF. Uh huh.

BARBARA. (*Rising.*) Clark, maybe you should wait for a lawyer. You're under a lot of pressure here, and ...

CLARK. No! I can tell this story! This was an accident, and I'm explaining how it happened. I'm cooperating with the police!

SHERIFF. And doing a damn fine job. You go right on.

BARBARA. But ...

HAMILTON. Barbara, let him talk.

BARBARA. But he's only going to get deeper in ...

CLARK. Barbara, shut up! Dammit! I want to cooperate with the police!

(BARBARA, hurt, turns away.)

CLARK. So. We had this new scene which we did put together rather quickly, but it was a good scene, really, I liked it, and it would've had a major effect on everything else in the picture, so ...

SHERIFF. Damn! "Picture" is a movie, too, isn't it? That's *three*! Why do you reckon they call it so many different things?

CLARK. Um, well, I don't know. I never really thought about it.

SHERIFF. Yep, I know, most people don't, but I think about that kind of thing all the time. Drives Buck crazy. Sorry.

CLARK. No, that's okay. It's interesting. (*To Hamilton.*) It is.

SHERIFF. Go ahead.

CLARK. Ah ... well ... we had this new scene, the final scene of the ... uh, story, and, basically, what we wanted to do was get Derek to kill himself.

(HAMILTON reacts with another coughing fit.)

CLARK. In the movie! The picture! His character! You see, Derek's character is named Howard Howard Lawton, and he's been swindled out of everything by the Howards, and he's so destroyed by all the corruption in his life, we decided he should just end up ... killing himself. See? So, we put Uncle Norton in the big chair, and ...

SHERIFF. Wup. Hold it. How'd your uncle get into all this? And where is he now? (*The SHERIFF pulls his gun and heads up the stairs, looking for Uncle Norton.*)

CLARK. Oh, no, no! He's not *my* uncle! There is no Uncle Norton, really, not in real life, it's Norton Howard, he's a character in the movie. He was never really here. I made him up.

SHERIFF. You made him up? Then who did you put in the big chair?

CLARK. Nobody! Well, nobody at first. What I mean is, Uncle Norton is in the scene where Howard Howard kills himself, but he's already dead, or rather Howard Howard kills him in the course of the action, but he's not really featured, so for the purposes of blocking out the scene, we just placed him in the big chair ... (*Beat.*) This is really much simpler than it sounds.

SHERIFF. I reckon it must be. Let me see. You wanted to just block out this scene altogether, so you picked up somebody's dead uncle who wasn't really here and sat him in the big chair so this fellow with the two first names could use him for target practice? Is that about it?

CLARK. NO! Well, sort of. Look, none of this so far is really all that important, EXCEPT that *Derek* ... (*Points to bloody rug.*) ... was pretending to be *Uncle Norton* ... (*Points to big chair.*) ... when the gun went off, (*Points to imaginary pistol in his hand.*) ... so you see, not only was it an accident that the gun was loaded, I wasn't really even aiming at *Derek,* I was aiming at *Uncle Norton,* for God's sake, for the purposes of the scene. See? I was sort of showing Derek how he should do it with this fancy gun that he had already checked to be empty ... Oh! Did I mention that he checked the gun himself?

(The SHERIFF shakes his head. CLARK acts out the following scenario with great animation, playing all the parts.)

CLARK. Oh! Well, that's important. That's *very* important. See, Derek wanted to use a real gun for the rehearsal, but we said "Oh, no, Derek, too dangerous, don't do it," but he said "Hey, man, I will if I want to,"—that's the way he was—and then he got the pistol from the governor's case, and we said "Oh, my goodness, Derek, be careful," so he checked to make sure it was empty, we watched him and everything, and we said "Derek, are you sure that's empty?" and he said "Yep, empty!" So. Imagine my surprise when Hamilton said "Show him what you want, Clark," and while I was showing him, him being Derek being Uncle Norton, the gun just ... went off.

(Pause. The SHERIFF stares at Clark.)

CLARK. Bang. (*Pause.*) Just imagine. (*Pause.*) I was ... shocked. (*Pause.*) I guess that's why I passed out.

BARBARA. (*Goes to Clark, takes his hand.*) Clark. Honey. I know you're scared. And I know you don't want me to interfere. But if you really feel you have to talk to this man tonight, I think it's better if you just tell the truth.

CLARK. What???

BARBARA. Well, I'm sure they'll take your history into consideration, and ...

CLARK. Barbara, what are you talking about??

BARBARA. Clark, honey, Hamilton told me the whole story.

CLARK. He ... What whole story? (*HE turns to Hamilton.*) Hamilton? What did you tell her?

HAMILTON. Just the truth, Clark. I thought you'd want it that way.

CLARK. What truth? What's going on?

SHERIFF. All right. I was wondering when somebody was going to stop the bull. Thank you, ma'am. Now, cuz, you want to go back and tell me what really happened?

CLARK. What do you mean what really happened? That is what really happened! Hamilton?

HAMILTON. Clark, I wish I could help you. You know I'd do anything for you. But Barbara's right. I mean, temporary insanity, anybody could understand that. The names Derek called you when we were going over the changes, it could almost be justifiable homicide. And with your history ....

CLARK. Stop about my history, for God's sake! And what do you mean the names Derek called me ... What about our scene, the final scene, and ... (*CLARK stops suddenly.*) Oh, wait a minute ...

HAMILTON. Sheriff ...

CLARK. Wait a minute. Oh, my God. Oh, my God! (*CLARK leaps at Hamilton, grabs him by the throat.*)

BARBARA. Doodles!

CLARK. You set me up! All that business about our "art"! You were setting me up!!

SHERIFF. (*Pulls Clark off of Hamilton.*) Easy, son, easy!

CLARK. Don't you get it? He's lying! He wanted to get Derek out of the way, he was supposed to switch the pistols, but the son of a bitch double crossed me!

SHERIFF. Calm down, son. Get hold of yourself before I have to pop you up side the head. What do you mean, switch the pistols?

CLARK. The pistols! The pistols were identical, and that's why it would work! All right. I've got to tell the truth now, the real story. I *was* lying before, but now I have to tell the truth. (*HE turns to Barbara.*) Barbara, what did he tell you? What did he say about the changes, and Derek? And the pistols?

BARBARA. Clark ...

CLARK. Tell me, dammit!

BARBARA. He told me what happened, Clark. How you exploded when Derek told you what he wanted to change in the screenplay, how he insulted your writing, how you grabbed the governor's pistol ...

CLARK. Oh, God. Oh, God, no. It's all a lie! He's lying!

BARBARA. But Clark, I heard the shouting, and I saw you with the gun! That's why I was so desperate for Hamilton to let me in. I just had a feeling something tragic was going to happen. And Clark, I saw you shoot him!

CLARK. Yes! Yes, I know! But don't you see, it was all part of Hamilton's plan! His plot! To get Derek out of the way! And to get me out of the way, too!

SHERIFF. Wup! Hold it! You're changing your whole story now? So I should just forget all that stuff about your uncle and the corruption and the boy with the two first names?

CLARK. Yes! No! I mean, don't forget it, it was all part of his plot to frame me!! Don't you see? Hamilton set up the whole thing. It makes perfect sense. He's a *director*! That's what he does! He figured out this whole business with the script, the final scene, so that Derek ...

SHERIFF. I thought you two worked out that last scene together.

CLARK. Well, we did, I thought we did, but I see now, he did all the talking, really, I just, I just ...

(Pause.)

SHERIFF. You just what?

CLARK. ... Went along ... oh, my God, I just went along. I went along. (*CLARK breaks down.*)

HAMILTON. Clark. Listen to me. There is no scene. There was a fight. Between you and Derek. It was real life. It happened. You've got to try to understand that. There is no scene.

CLARK. Don't patronize me, you son of a bitch! There's no scene because you destroyed it. That was part of the plot, too, you see? (*HE looks up suddenly.*) The computer! He typed it into the computer! (*HE rushes to the desk and switches on the computer.*) If he typed it in, it has to be here! Where's the disk? (*HE checks the computer's disk drive, pulls out a disk.*) Oh, thank God, it's still here! (*HE shoves the disk back in the computer.*) Now, what would he call it? Uh ...

HAMILTON. (*Jumps up, goes to the computer.*) Clark, you're raving! Officer, haven't you heard enough?

CLARK. (*Pushes him away.*) Shut up! Get away from me! (*Reading from computer screen.*) Budget.doc, Letters.doc, Locations.doc, Endscene.doc ... Endscene.doc! That's it! (*HE punches some keys on the computer, reads the first few lines on the screen.*) This is it! Thank God! (*HE jumps up and pulls the SHERIFF to the desk.*) Look! Look! Read this! Read it!

SHERIFF. (*Goes to the computer, sits, and reads.*) "Cut to the Howard Plantation Study. Howard Howard is pacing. His uncle, Norton Howard, is laughing softly in the big chair ..."

CLARK. You see?

SHERIFF. "Suddenly Howard Howard stops pacing, reaches into his coat..."

CLARK. You see? You see?

SHERIFF. "... and pulls out a leather-bound checkbook."

CLARK. What?

SHERIFF. "He whips a pen from an engraved, brass desk set on the desk and begins to write a check..."

CLARK. Wait a minute! Let me see that! "... and begins to write a check for the full value of the plantation ..." What?? This isn't it! This ... Oh, my God! He must've switched the disks! Like he was supposed to switch the pistols. He switched the disks! Why? Because he *hates* me ... why does he hate me? Because of Barbara! Of course! Because we had an affair! Barbara, you told him, didn't you? You told him about our affair! That's it! My God, there's your motive right there! Tell him, Barbara! Don't you see? He's lying to you, too! He hates us both! Tell him. Tell the sheriff we had an affair!

SHERIFF. Well? Did you?

BARBARA. (*Taps her temple and shakes her head sadly.*) In his mind ...

CLARK. What?

(BARBARA looks at Clark with great pity.)

CLARK. Oh, no ... Not you. Not you, too!

SHERIFF. (*Taking out handcuffs.*) Cuz, we'd better go into town.

CLARK. No! Wait! This is wrong, it's all wrong! I'm not crazy! Really!

SHERIFF. I know. I know. Never said you were. Let's go. (*HE handcuffs Clark's hands behind his back and leads him to the door, then turns to Hamilton and Barbara.*) I'd like to thank you both for your cooperation. Sorry to keep you up so late.

HAMILTON. Perfectly all right.

BARBARA. Please ... be gentle with him. He really is a good man. We never should have put him under this strain.

CLARK. Barbara ...

BARBARA. Oh, Clark ... why did you do it? (*SHE bursts into tears and turns away.*)

CLARK. I ... I ...

SHERIFF. Let's go.

(CLARK looks from Barbara to Hamilton, speechless. HE starts to protest to the sheriff, but realizes it's no use. A broken man, HE turns and walks to the door.)

SHERIFF. Good night, everybody. You'll hear from me if I need you. (*HE escorts CLARK out the door. We hear his voice fade into the night as HE reads Clark his rights.*) Cuz, you have the right to remain silent. Anything you say can and will be used against you in a court of law. You have the right to an attorney ...

(HAMILTON goes to the door and locks it. BARBARA's crying stops abruptly. SHE walks to the window, looks after Clark and the Sheriff for a moment, then turns back to Hamilton. SHE reaches into the pocket of her robe, pulls out a computer disk, and "toasts" Hamilton with it, a smile slowly crossing her face. HAMILTON switches on the piano and begins to applaud, slowly at first, then faster and louder as the MUSIC plays and the LIGHTS fade to black.)

ACT II

Scene 2

Four hours later.

AT RISE: The stage is dark, except for a glimmer of MOONLIGHT that shines through the window, illuminating several empty champagne bottles and other evidence of a late night of celebrating. The house is quiet, except for the crash of the WAVES outside.

Suddenly there is a POUNDING on the door. Then silence. A LIGHT goes on upstairs. More POUNDING.

HAMILTON appears at the top of the stairs, tying his robe. HE is disheveled and clearly hung over. The POUNDING continues as HE descends the stairs.

HAMILTON. All right! All right! I'm coming!

(HAMILTON opens the door to the SHERIFF, who is dressed in gardening clothes.)

SHERIFF. I'm sorry, were you asleep?

HAMILTON. Yes! Yes, I was. What time is it?

SHERIFF. Oh, it's almost five o'clock. Thought sure you'd be up. I saw Barbara Walkers talking to some movie fellow once who was just carrying on about how the day started at four a.m. and sometimes went on way past midnight. Sometimes seven days a week. Is that not right?

HAMILTON. When we're shooting. Yes. Long hours, long days—When we're shooting. Not now. Not yet. Regular hours now. Come back later. Much later.

SHERIFF. Oh ... when you're *shooting*! I get it. Well, hold on. Tell you what. Since we're both up now, and we're both here, let's talk for just a tiny little bit, won't take but a second, really, and then you can go back to bed and sleep all day if you want to and I can get back to my garden and not have to make another trip. I'll even make us some of Skippy's coffee. What do you say?

BARBARA. (*Appears at the top of the stairs in a robe; groggy.*) Hamilton, who is it?

HAMILTON. It's the sheriff, Barbara. He's come to make us coffee.

BARBARA. What? Coffee?

SHERIFF. Be right back.

(HE exits to kitchen. BARBARA descends the stairs. HAMILTON and BARBARA begin to tidy up, hiding champagne bottles, etc.)

BARBARA. Hamilton, what is it? What's wrong?

HAMILTON. I don't know.

BARBARA. Well, why is he here?

HAMILTON. Barbara, I don't know. He's very strange. Just be calm. And remember how upset you are about Clark.

BARBARA. Of course. But ...

SHERIFF. (*Reenters.*) Got the pot going, won't be long now, hot java coming up. Morning, ma'am.

BARBARA. Morning.

HAMILTON. Are you always this perky at five a.m.?

SHERIFF. Perky? Perky. Huh. Well, yes, I suppose I am. Never thought about it. Do like mornings though. Everything's clearer in the morning. Perky.

BARBARA. Sheriff, what can we do for you? I assume this isn't a social call.

SHERIFF. No, well, you're right, not entirely, anyway. Although it is nice to see some new faces around here. Don't get much new blood. Wup. Poor choice of words. Excuse me.

HAMILTON. Yes. Well. I must admit, I'm a little curious, too, sheriff. Why *are* you here? Other than your overwhelming neighborly desire to be the first to wish us good morning?

SHERIFF. Well ... (*Pause. The SHERIFF begins to move about the room, looking at the computer, the pistol case, examining the evidence at the scene of the crime.*)

HAMILTON. What? Did Clark come up with another preposterous story?

SHERIFF. Oh, no, he pretty much stuck to that business about being framed. Didn't really talk about it all that much, actually, he seemed to be feeling pretty low, can't really blame him ... no, it's not him, it's, uh ... well...

HAMILTON. Yes?

SHERIFF. Skippy.

(*Pause.*)

HAMILTON.	BARBARA.
Skippy?	Skippy?

SHERIFF. Yes, ma'am, I got a message through to Skippy in Djakarta, and he's going to be calling me back at my office in just about an hour, and it's worrying me to death. He's going to hate this. He's just going to hate this whole thing.

HAMILTON. Yes, it's a terrible tragedy. Derek was a talented young man.

SHERIFF. Oh, Skippy won't care about the tragedy. He's just going to hate that it happened at his house! (*Confidentially.*) You see, there's an election coming up, and ...

HAMILTON. Say no more, we understand.

SHERIFF. (*Crossing to Hamilton.*) Well, good. I'm glad, because I'm going to have to lay out this whole business in a long distance, overseas telephone call, and thinking about it all out there with my tomatoes, I couldn't keep it quite straight. I need you to help me with one or two things, uh ... (*HE takes out his notebook.*) You see, I just have to make sure this all joints together, couple of things *you* said, ma'am ... (*HE turns to Barbara.*)

BARBARA. Me?

SHERIFF. Yes, ma'am, when your friend was having his fit, uh ... oh, yes, here ... made myself a few notes ...

(HE reads, mumbling to himself, shaking his head. BARBARA and HAMILTON exchange glances. Suddenly the SHERIFF snaps his book closed, sniffs the air, and looks up at Barbara quizzically.)

BARBARA. Yes?

SHERIFF. Coffee. Be right back. (*The SHERIFF hurries off to the kitchen.*)

BARBARA. Hamilton, what is he talking about? What did I say? Did I say anything wrong?

HAMILTON. I don't know. I don't think so. I thought you were marvelous.

BARBARA. I don't need a review, dammit, I need to know what the hell he's talking about!

HAMILTON. Well, don't get testy with me!

BARBARA. I'm sorry, darling, I just thought everything was going so well ...

HAMILTON. It is. And it'll all be over soon. *Be* upset. *Be* a little rattled. Everything shouldn't be too perfect, anyway. Just drink his coffee, answer his questions and we'll get him out of here as soon as possible.

BARBARA. Oh, God, I hope this is all worth it.

HAMILTON. Barbara look at me. Do you love me?

BARBARA. Yes.

HAMILTON. Do you hate Clark?

BARBARA. Yes.

HAMILTON. Would you like us to have an enormous amount of money all to ourselves?

BARBARA. Yes ...

HAMILTON. Then it's worth it. Sssh!

(The SHERIFF reenters from the kitchen, carrying a tray with coffee, cups, cream pitcher, sugar bowl, spoons, etc. HE sets the tray on the coffee table, sits on the sofa and begins pouring for the group.)

SHERIFF. Coffee wagon! All right. Mmmmm, I do love that smell. Skippy's got a little Columbian fellow, flies in here every few months on business, drops off a couple of big burlap sacks, can't get this at the A&P, I'll tell you what! All right, let's see now. How do you take yours? Ma'am?

BARBARA. That's all right, thank you, I'll do it, thank you.

HAMILTON. And just black for me, thanks.

(The SHERIFF sings the Maxwell House percolator theme as HE delivers a cup of coffee to Hamilton, then watches intently as BARBARA prepares her coffee and takes a sip.)

BARBARA. (*Genuinely.*) This is really very good.

SHERIFF. (*Slapping his knee.*) Ha! Ha! Didn't I tell you? Oh, I love a good cup of coffee! Wish I had a biscuit, though ... (*The SHERIFF starts to head for the kitchen again.)*

HAMILTON. Sheriff! Was there something specific you wanted to ask my wife?

SHERIFF. Oh! Yes, yes, there was ... three things, actually, let's see, let me just jot this down as we go along, here ... (*HE takes out his note pad again, shuffles through it.*) All right, here, here ... you were out on the beach before the shooting, that's what you said, didn't you?

BARBARA. Yes. That's correct. I had gone for a swim while they were meeting to talk about the film.

SHERIFF. Uh, huh. Uh, huh. I got that, that's just what I wrote down, right here. All right. Then, you came in just a tiny second before the fatal shot, *witnessed* it, saw it happen, bang, right there, right in front of you, is that right?

BARBARA. Yes. It was horrible. I was stunned.

SHERIFF. Oh, yes, I can imagine. Awful thing, to see somebody shot. Awful.

BARBARA. Yes. Yes, it is.

SHERIFF. Why'd you come in?

BARBARA. What?

SHERIFF. Why'd you come in? From your swim? *Right then?*

BARBARA. Well ... I was cold ... The sun was going down ... uh ...

SHERIFF. (*Suddenly the SHERIFF gets an a idea.*) Were you wet?

BARBARA. Yes! I was wet, I was cold, I wanted in.

SHERIFF. Good! There you go! (*Scribbles in notebook.*) Cold, *wet*, wanted in ... *that's* better! (*Goes back to reading his notes.*) And so you "knocked on the door, and just as Mr. Orr let you in ..." Oh! Why was the door locked?

BARBARA. Why...?

SHERIFF. You went out for a swim, and when you came back, cold and wet, you had to knock to get in. Door must've been locked. Why was that?

BARBARA. Well, because ... I don't know. (*Turns to Hamilton.*) Why was the door locked?

HAMILTON. (*Calmly.*) I locked the door so we wouldn't be disturbed during our meeting.

BARBARA. Yes. Of course. That's not unusual, is it? Men stuff. You know. God knows what goes on behind closed doors in these high powered movie meetings of theirs. No girls allowed. Like a club. *(SHE is about to begin one of her extended metaphors.*) Like a club house ...

HAMILTON. Barbara ...

BARBARA. Yes. All right. So. I came in from the beach because I was cold, and wet, and they had locked me out so they could have a private meeting. Anything else?

SHERIFF. Well. Let's see. Ummm ...

HAMILTON. Sheriff, it's really an open and shut case, isn't it? Crime of passion by an unbalanced artist, in front of two witnesses, a history of animosity between the perpetrator and the victim ...

SHERIFF. Whoa, whoa, slow down, that's good, that's very good, let me get all that—"history of animosity, perpetrator and the victim"—that's damn good, I'll definitely use that, sounds like a movie ...

HAMILTON. Well, it's not a movie, sheriff, it's real life, and we're all very sorry it happened, but I'm beginning to feel the stress of the past twenty-four hours, and I'm sure my wife is exhausted, so if there's nothing else ...

SHERIFF. Right, sorry, almost done. Just, uh ... oh, yes. You said "Clark, I saw you with the gun ..."

BARBARA. Yes! Yes, I did, of course, I told you I witnessed the whole thing ...

SHERIFF. Wup. Hold it, I know, let me finish here. You said "I saw you with the gun, that's why I was so desperate for Hamilton to let me in." How'd you see the gun before he let you in?

BARBARA. (*Pause. BARBARA looks to the door.*) The window! On the porch! I ... I heard shouting as I was coming up the beach, I ran up to the porch, I peered in the window, and there was Clark just ... brandishing this pistol and screaming. At Derek. It was frightening. I'd never seen him like that. That's when I started pounding on the door ...

SHERIFF. Because you "had the feeling something tragic was going to happen." Yep. Got it, that's exactly what you said next. (*Writing.*) "Through the *window*. Brandishing pistol and screaming." All right! You see, that's the kind of details Skippy will definitely want to hear, especially without a confession. Good. I think that's all. Let's see. Beach. Cold and wet. Shouting. Porch. Window. Pistol. Pounding. In. Bang. Good. Got it. (*HE snaps notebook shut, stands, points toward the beach, then to the big chair, the window, the door, and again to the big chair, nodding.*) Got it. Good. Thank you. Thank you very much for your time. Hope you enjoyed the coffee, there's more in the pot, shouldn't have to trouble you any further. (*HE goes to the door, stops, takes business cards from his pocket, and gives one to each of them.*) All the same, I'd appreciate it if you wouldn't leave the vicinity without letting me know. Just give a holler to Buck down at the station, let him know any travel plans. Just as a little legal courtesy. You know how the courts are these days .... Have a good one.

(And HE is out the door. We hear his FOOTSTEPS leaving the porch and heading for the dock. BARBARA collapses onto the sofa.)

BARBARA. Oh God. Oh God. That was awful. What if I'd been on a witness stand? The gun, the window ... do you think he believed me?

HAMILTON. (*Tearing up the sheriff s card.*) of course he believed you, darling, he's an idiot! He wasn't trying to trip you up, you heard what he said, he just needed a tight script to read to Governor Bob.

BARBARA. (*Going to him.*) I just ... I got so confused! Hamilton, I'm so sorry I knocked on the door too soon yesterday. I heard you say "run the scene again" and I thought you were ready for me! I could've ruined everything.

HAMILTON. Yes, but you didn't. We got right back on track and it all came off perfectly.

BARBARA. But it confused me! Today! Talking to the sheriff! And then that business about not leaving town! He's suspicious of us, Hamilton, I know he is. He suspects we did plot against Clark.

HAMILTON. Barbara, he doesn't.

(HAMILTON puts his arm around her and THEY head for the stairs.)

HAMILTON. Come on, baby, we're right on schedule. Don't get worked up over nothing.

(Suddenly there is POUNDING on the door. HAMILTON and BARBARA freeze. THEY look at each other, then HAMILTON goes to the door and opens it to the sheriff.)

HAMILTON. Yes?

SHERIFF. Excuse me again. Sorry. Just one more question. Do you mind?

HAMILTON. What is it?

SHERIFF. Can I come in? That's not the question, but can I? Come in?

HAMILTON. Oh. Sorry. Certainly.

(The SHERIFF enters, nodding to Barbara. SHE smiles weakly.)

HAMILTON. What's the question?

SHERIFF. Well ....What does a director do?

(Pause.)

HAMILTON. What?

SHERIFF. A director. On a movie. What does he do?

HAMILTON. You want to know what a director does? That's the question?

SHERIFF. Yep. Never could figure that out.

HAMILTON. (*Shaking his head.*) Never could figure that out ....

SHERIFF. But you're a director, right? So what do you do, exactly?

HAMILTON. (*Exploding.*) This is preposterous!

BARBARA. Darling ...

HAMILTON. No! It's unconscionable! You roust me out of bed at four-thirty in the morning after what promises to be the most traumatic night of my life, you grill my wife with a notebook full of dim-witted detective questions. And now you have the gall to expect me to continue your ... remedial course in motion picture terminology???

SHERIFF. Well don't go getting all huffy ...

HAMILTON. I damn well will get "huffy"! Now you listen to me, sheriff. My wife and I are law abiding citizens who have had the great misfortune to witness the mental breakdown and consequent tragic behavior of an emotionally deranged colleague. We have made every effort to indulge your pastoral peculiarities. But I'll be damned if I'll submit to any more of your idiotic inquisition unless it relates directly to the case!

SHERIFF. (*After a moment.*) Are you done?

HAMILTON. Completely.

SHERIFF. All right. What does a director do?

HAMILTON. Are you deaf? I just said ...

SHERIFF. IT RELATES DIRECTLY TO THE CASE! (*HE whips out his notebook and flips to a page.*) Right here! Quote: "Don't you see? Hamilton set up the whole thing! It makes perfect sense. He's a director! That's what he does!"

HAMILTON. Oh. I see. Well, I ... I'm sorry.

SHERIFF. Don't tell me you're sorry, just tell me what a director does so I can make some sense out of that statement when I read it to Skippy! What does a director do?

HAMILTON. Ah, he, uh, he ... everything! He does everything! He casts the actors, he refines the script, he chooses locations, he sets up shots ... basically, he structures the logical and emotional progression of the entire picture.

SHERIFF. He what?

BARBARA. Darling? Sheriff, let's say a movie is a big church picnic.

HAMILTON. Barbara ...

BARBARA. (*Acting out the scenario.*) No, no, let me finish, he'll understand this. Say it's a big picnic at your church. Now, if I parachuted out of a plane and discreetly landed in the middle of the picnic, I'd see people laughing and eating and dancing—if your particular denomination allows dancing ... Anyway, it would all be happening, seemingly without rhyme or reason, before my eyes, very spontaneous, just everyone all together in good fellowship, having a good time. BUT! What I *wouldn't* see is your little country pastor, up at dawn, mowing the grass at the picnic site, setting up the tables, starting the fires for the bar-be-cues, or his little country wife, up all night baking pies and frying chicken ... both of them, getting everything ready so the day will run smoothly and everyone else can enjoy themselves. The director of a movie is like that little country couple ... do you understand? (*BARBARA finishes her analogy standing beside Hamilton in an American Gothic pose, using a coffee spoon as a pitchfork.*)

SHERIFF. (*Thoughtfully.*) Huh. So basically, you just get everybody set up, turn 'em loose, then sit back and pray to the good Lord that it doesn't rain?

HAMILTON. No! Good work, Barbara.

SHERIFF. So what do you think he meant, then, "he's a director, that's what he does"?

HAMILTON. I have no earthly idea.

SHERIFF. (*Shrugs his shoulders.*) Then I guess we better ask him. Be right back. (*HE heads for the door.*)

HAMILTON. Ask him? Wait a minute, where are you going? Where's Clark?

SHERIFF. Oh, I handcuffed him down to the dock. See, I was showing him my tomatoes when I got to thinking about all this, and I didn't want to waste time going all the way back to the jail. (*Looks at watch.*) And, oh my goodness, I promised him coffee and totally forgot. (*Starts for the pot; stops.*) Well, he can have it when he gets here, I guess. Save him some, will you? Be right back.

(*The SHERIFF exits. BARBARA follows him to the door, looks out the window toward the dock, then turns back to Hamilton.*)

BARBARA. Hamilton, I can't face Clark! I can't!

HAMILTON. Barbara ...

BARBARA. No! It's too much! I can't look him in the face. When we started this, I ... I thought I hated him, he'd hurt me so badly, but now ... seeing him ...

HAMILTON. "But now seeing him" what?

BARBARA. I don't know! I don't know anything any more.

HAMILTON. (*Going to her.*) Barbara, what is the matter with you? You can't fall apart on me now! Half of this was your idea, hell, more than half!

BARBARA. It was not!

HAMILTON. Hey. I wanted to get rid of Derek, you said you hated Clark so much you could kill him. Sounds like a fair balance to me!

BARBARA. I know, but ... Damn you, Hamilton, damn you! It's all your fault! I should be plotting to kill *you*!

HAMILTON. What? What's my fault?

BARBARA. This! This crazy, awful ... The way I feel! The way I've felt for the past year! You used me like a common whore to get Clark out of the way so you could re-cut your stupid movie!

HAMILTON. Barbara, I told you to keep him occupied. I never suggested you do it in bed.

BARBARA. You knew I was attracted to him! You left us alone together in the most romantic setting possible! You must have known we'd have an affair.

HAMILTON. (*After a moment.*) Yes. But I didn't know you'd have the exceedingly bad taste to fall in love with him.

BARBARA. You bastard!

HAMILTON. No, darling. A bastard is the lover who throws his mistress out into the street. Not the caring husband who takes her back when she comes groveling home.

(BARBARA slaps Hamilton. SHE would slap him again but HE grabs her hand, bending back her arm and forcing her to her knees.)

BARBARA. Hamilton, you're hurting me!

HAMILTON. Listen to me, my love. I don't know what sort of maternal instincts that pathetic little man has re-kindled in you, but I suggest we continue to work together until Clark is behind bars, the sheriff is satisfied, and this all fades away like a bad dream. Don't you think that would be best?

BARBARA. (*In pain.*) Yes. Yes, dammit. Let me go.

(The door opens and CLARK enters, in handcuffs, followed by the SHERIFF. CLARK glares at Hamilton with great hatred.)

SHERIFF. Oh. Excuse me. We should've knocked.

HAMILTON. (*Helping BARBARA up.*) Ho, up we go. Easy now. Are you all right, darling? She took a bit of a spill on her way to the loo. Did you twist your ankle?

BARBARA. No. No, I'm fine. Thank you ... darling. (*SHE rushes up the stairs.*)

CLARK. (*Hissing at Hamilton.*) Liar.

SHERIFF. Hey!

CLARK. Traitor.

SHERIFF. Stop that!

CLARK. Judas.

SHERIFF. Now stop that, I said, or I'll trot you right back down to that dock. Sit down here while I get you some coffee.

(The SHERIFF seats CLARK in the armchair, then goes to pour him a cup of coffee. CLARK hisses at Hamilton behind the sheriff s back.)

CLARK. Slime.

HAMILTON. (*Calmly.*) Psycho.

CLARK. (*Exploding and rushing wildly at Hamilton.*) Hollywood Hitler harlot!

SHERIFF. (*Rushes to pull Clark off Hamilton.*) Hey! Hey! Hey! All right, that's it, that's enough! I'm not going to have any of that here, you understand me? Like a little kid, I swear. Come on. (*HE hauls CLARK to the stairs and handcuffs him to the banister.*) From now on, anything you have to say to him, you say it through me, is that understood?

CLARK. Yes. I'm sorry.

SHERIFF. All right. And *you* ... (*Turns back to Hamilton.*) Give me your hand.

HAMILTON. Me??

SHERIFF. (*Takes a second pair of handcuffs from his belt.*) Yes, you, I heard you call him a psycho. I'm liking you less and less as the morning wears on. Give me your hand.

HAMILTON. No, no, no, that won't be necessary ...

SHERIFF. Give me your hand!!

(HAMILTON reluctantly holds out his hand. The SHERIFF clasps a handcuff to his wrist, and the other to the leg of the piano [or any available railing, handle, etc., on the set that provides suitable distance from Clark.])

SHERIFF. Now. Maybe that'll serve to keep you two separated in case I have to turn my back on you again for two seconds. A couple of grown men, you'd think this was Romper Room. (*HE turns to Clark.*) How do you take your coffee, cuz?

CLARK. Oh. Uh, just milk, thanks.

(The SHERIFF goes back to preparing Clark's coffee. BARBARA appears at the top of the stairs, dabbing her eyes with a Kleenex. SHE sees Clark and screams.)

BARBARA. Aaahhh! What...??? (*SHE looks down the stairs and sees Hamilton in handcuffs.*) Oh, my God! What happened? What's happening?

SHERIFF. Just trying to maintain a civil atmosphere here, ma'am. Now, do you think *you* can behave yourself on your own? I'm afraid I've run out of restraining devices.

BARBARA. Yes ... yes, of course.

SHERIFF. Good. Then would you sit down over there, please? Thank you.

(BARBARA sits. The SHERIFF hands CLARK a cup and saucer of coffee. CLARK stares at it for a moment, at a loss how to drink it because of his handcuffs. The SHERIFF begins to pace.)

SHERIFF. Now listen to me, folks. I am running out of time. I've got a bloody murder in the residence of the highest public official in the state, and at least three different stories as to how it happened, all of them more full of holes than the spout on my old tin watering can.

CLARK. My *second* story's not full of holes!

SHERIFF. Hush! Now, Skippy is breathing down my neck for a confession, and if I don't get one for him, I've got to at least hand him a story that makes a little bit of sense. Cuz, I'll tell you the truth, I'd like to believe you. I would. You seem like a nice young fellow, and you've got people in Wiggins. But so far, there's not a damn thing you've said to help me along here! So I don't care any more what a director does, or why this movie star or that one would be good or not good for your "film," or why you'd make up an uncle you never even had and pretend he's sitting in the damn room while you take up a pistol and blow a partner of yours away! If you're not going to confess to the thing the way he says it happened, I've got to have some hard proof that he's lying and I've got to know why! (*HE takes out his pocket watch and holds it up to Clark.*) Now. You've got five minutes. Tell me what I should ask him.

HAMILTON. Wait a minute. I don't have to submit to a second hand interrogation from that ...

SHERIFF. (*Wheels on Hamilton.*) You want to run this show? Huh? Do you? Because you can! Yessir, I'll let you run the whole damn thing this morning. But by God, you won't be running things when that gavel bangs in Judge Melvin's court, and all three of you are up on charges of murder, conspiring to commit a felony, obstructing justice, and ... and defacing taxpayer's property!

(*HE indicates the bloody rug and armchair.*) So do you want to run things here this morning???

(*HAMILTON shakes his head. The SHERIFF yells in his face like a drill sergeant.*)

SHERIFF. I DIDN'T HEAR YOU!!

HAMILTON. No! Sorry! You're doing a fine job!

SHERIFF. (*Sweetly.*) Thank you. (*HE holds up his watch to Clark.*) All right. Five minutes.

CLARK. (*Setting down his coffee.*) Okay. Okay. Five minutes? Okay. You want to know *why* he's lying? Hm? Why they're both lying through their teeth? Okay. Make them tell you about me and Barbara.

BARBARA. (*Patronizing.*) Clark ...

CLARK. No! Don't tell him it was just "in my mind"! I'll get proof! When we stayed on at that Inn across the river from Vicksburg, after Hamilton sneaked back to Hollywood to do his hatchet job on my film? The desk clerk, the night clerk who had to come and tell us to hold it down because I was moaning too loud and you were screaming "Oh, God, oh, God, kill me, kill me, it's heaven, it's heaven ..."

HAMILTON. What???

CLARK. Shut up! That desk clerk's name was Leon Strunk! He'll remember us, and sheriff, you can call him at the Mole Creek Inn in Tallulah, Louisiana any time between midnight and eight a.m. and ask him. And if he's not there you ask to speak to Lounez, she's a maid, she walked in on us once when I was tied to the bed all covered with Cool Whip and Barbara was wearing this ...

BARBARA. (*Leaping up.*) Clark! Sheriff, I ... I'm afraid I have a confession to make.

CLARK. Ha!

HAMILTON. Barbara ...

BARBARA. No. I'm sorry, darling, I know these aren't the best circumstances for you to hear this, but ... well ... it's true. Clark and I did have a brief ... liaison. But it didn't mean anything! Really! It was just ... circumstantial.

CLARK. Oh, please!

SHERIFF. Hush, now, let her talk.

BARBARA. Sheriff, what can I say? These things happen. But Clark and I parted as friends. There was no animosity between us. And I never told Hamilton because it really had nothing to do with our relationship, nothing at all, and well, I guess I wanted to protect him. You understand, don't you? Say a marriage is ... an oxygen tent. Now ...

SHERIFF.	CLARK.
All right, yes, I got it, I understand.	No, no, Barbara, that's okay.

(BARBARA sits.)

HAMILTON. Barbara, I don't know what to say! I'm shocked!

CLARK. No he's not! Sheriff, he's not shocked! He knew! She told him!

BARBARA. I did not!

CLARK. You did! It didn't mean "nothing" to her, sheriff! She wanted to leave him and move in with me, but I said no! So they framed me because they both hate me!

HAMILTON. That's a paranoid delusion!

CLARK. No it isn't! I figured it all out in jail last night! She told him and he took her back, but he *had* to be jealous, because she said that after making love with me, making love with him would be like going to the dentist!

BARBARA. I never said that! Darling, I would never ...

CLARK. You said it to *me*!

HAMILTON. You did???

SHERIFF. All right ...

CLARK. And he's a greedy, arrogant little man who can't stand any competition and has to be the boss ...

HAMILTON. (*To the sheriff.*) Not true! Not true!

CLARK. ... and setting me up to kill Derek would get us both out of the way and make him—whoop-de-do—*president* of the Three Happy Fellows ...

HAMILTON. I didn't need to be president, I was already the only one with any ...

CLARK. ... and he could collect *all* the profits from *both* movies, and not have anybody around any more to remind him that even his wife knows what a pathetic weasel he really is!

SHERIFF. All right, I said!

HAMILTON. You sanctimonious, smart ass wacko! Do you really expect anybody to believe she'd choose you over me?

CLARK. She did! She did!

HAMILTON. Hell, I paid for your motel room!! I didn't give a damn if you slept with her, you were just picking through my leftover garbage!

BARBARA. (*Leaps to her feet.*) You little-dicked son of a bitch! Don't you call me garbage!

HAMILTON. Garbage! Garbage!

SHERIFF. Hey!
BARBARA. Pig!
HAMILTON. Slut!
SHERIFF. Hey, now!
BARBARA. Sadist!!
CLARK. Murderers!!!
HAMILTON. Lunatic!!!!
BARBARA. BAAASTAAARDS!!!!!

(Exasperated, the SHERIFF takes out his pistol and fires a shot into the ceiling. The NOISE abruptly silences the group. The SHERIFF looks up at the hole in the ceiling, then turns on the group in amazement and disgust.)

SHERIFF. God Almighty! I have never heard such a bunch of ugly talking people in my life! What do you think this is, a porn show? Your time is up, cuz, and as far as I'm concerned, you wasted it!

CLARK. But it's all true! It's motivation! The inn in Tallulah ... the maid ... the night clerk ... they saw us ...

SHERIFF. Cuz, I don't care if you got laid in a chicken costume on the buffet table at the Holiday Inn.

(CLARK reacts.)

SHERIFF. Doesn't prove a thing!

HAMILTON. Hah!

SHERIFF. (*Wheels on Hamilton.*) Shut up! You just shut your mouth! You think you're so damn smart! Well, you're not smart! I don't like you even a little bit. But! I believed you!

HAMILTON. You did?

SHERIFF. Yes, I believed you! This boy's story is a mess! But yours ... yours was clean and neat and easy! He didn't have a damn thing on you. All I had to do was tidy up a couple of little details, get him in here, let him speak his piece, show him how hopeless things were for him, and maybe, just maybe he would've signed this confession! (*HE whips out a typewritten sheet and waves it in Hamilton's face.*) No investigation, no trial, one quick bang of the gavel and everybody goes on about their business. (*HE slams the paper down on the desk in disgust.*) But no. You had to get sucked up into the name calling and the dirty talk and the bull. Well, to hell with you! To hell with all of you! (*HE looks at his watch.*) Damn! Well, I'll tell you what *I'm* going to do. I'm going down to the dock, I'm going to get Buck on the phone, and I'm going to tell him to clean out two more cells, because I am navigating back across the bay with *three* suspects to be held without bail, because I firmly believe they are *all* equally guilty of pre-meditated, first degree murder, for which, as he knows very well, the penalty in this state is DEATH! (*HE storms to the door.*) I'll be back.

(HE storms out, slamming the door, hard. CLARK, BARBARA, and HAMILTON stare after him for a long moment. Finally CLARK breaks the silence.)

CLARK. He seems pretty angry.

BARBARA. Yes, he does.

CLARK. Things look pretty bad.

HAMILTON. For you.

CLARK. For all of us.

HAMILTON. Hmph.

CLARK. Hamilton. How would you feel about ... okay, okay, wait a minute. (*CLARK closes his eyes and takes a few deep breaths to gather his power.*)

HAMILTON. Jesus.

CLARK. (*Opens his eyes and looks intently at Hamilton.*) Okay. How would you feel about making a deal?

HAMILTON. What?

CLARK. A deal. With me. Okay. Okay. I am going to prison. I know that. Or to an institution that will feel like prison. And that's right. I should go to prison. You wanted to kill Derek, and you made me want to kill Derek. But no matter how you manipulated me, I could've pulled out. I could've stopped it. But I didn't. I went along. And now Derek's dead. And his blood is on my hands.

HAMILTON. Oh, please, spare me.

CLARK. Shut up. His blood is on my hands. And I'll have to live with these bloody hands for the rest of my life. I know that. And it's horrible. But there's something I want. From you.

HAMILTON. And what might that be?

CLARK. (*Quietly.*) I want my movie.

(*Pause.*)

HAMILTON. You want your movie?

CLARK. Yes. I want my movie. The way I saw it in my head when I wrote it. I want to hear my words exactly the way I wrote them. I want William Putnam to play the character I modeled after my grandfather. If that can happen, I don't care what happens to you. But I have to know with absolute certainty that *you* will never, never, never, never, NEVER lay a finger on my work again, or see a dime from it. So. To get that assurance, I'm willing to make a deal. I'm willing to forget the way things really happened, sign that confession, and go to prison ... If you'll sign this. (*CLARK takes a couple of rumpled, typewritten sheets from his pocket.*)

HAMILTON. What the hell is that?

CLARK. It's an agreement. I typed it up in my cell last night on the sheriff's old Olivetti. It states that for "personal reasons," you are withdrawing from participation in *Three Happy Fellows, Inc.* and relinquishing any and all claims to the work of Clark Robinson, or any current or future deals based thereon. To put it in your language, Hamilton, it "cuts you out of the loop," once and for all. You sign this, I'll sign the confession. No trial, no investigation. (*Holds up the agreement.*) You want to make a deal?

(Pause. HAMILTON glares at Clark.)

BARBARA. Hamilton! Do it! For God's sake, it's only a movie!

HAMILTON. Shut up, Barbara! Why the hell would I make that kind of a deal with you, Clark? You heard the sheriff. Your story is a mess! So why would I want to make a deal with you?

CLARK. Because there's one thing I didn't tell the sheriff to ask you about.

HAMILTON. What?

CLARK. The bullet.

HAMILTON. The dud? Hah! It's in the Gulf of Mexico, Clark. You know, that large body of water just beyond the dock?

CLARK. Not the dud, Hamilton. The bullet that killed Derek. The bullet whose empty casing is still in Skippy's revolver. The revolver that will be people's Exhibit A if this goes to trial.

HAMILTON. What about it?

CLARK. That bullet casing has my fingerprints on it.

HAMILTON. So?

CLARK. *So* when did I touch it? If the gun was loaded, and I grabbed it in a fit of passion, and shot Derek before you could stop me, when did I handle the bullet?

HAMILTON. You handled it when ... when ...

CLARK. Come on, Hamilton. You're the director. When would I handle the bullet? Hm? Unless I loaded it myself. And when did I have time to do that? Your story is coming apart, Hamilton. Pull that one tiny thread and your story starts to come apart like an old moth-eaten sweater.

HAMILTON. No! That's ridiculous! There wouldn't be any fingerprints on that bullet casing. They'd ... they'd be burned off when the gun was fired! ... Wouldn't they?

CLARK. Do you want to take that chance?

(Pause.)

BARBARA. Hamilton, don't be an idiot! This isn't a movie! You can't just say "that's a wrap, let's go home." This is real. Real jail. Real bars. Give it up! Sign the paper!

(HAMILTON stares at the paper in Clark's hand for a moment, then looks down at his hand and the handcuffs.)

CLARK. Well?

(Pause.)

BARBARA. SIGN THE PAPER, HAMILTON!!!

(Long pause.)

HAMILTON. (*Quietly.*) Bring it to me.

(BARBARA rushes to Clark, grabs the agreement, and brings it to Hamilton. HAMILTON takes it from her, glances at it, glares back at Clark.)

HAMILTON. Take him the confession. And a pen.

(BARBARA grabs a pen from the desk, snatches up the confession, and takes it to Clark. SHE goes back to Hamilton. THEY both look at Clark.)

HAMILTON. Sign it.

CLARK. Not until you sign that first.

HAMILTON. I'm not signing first. How do I know you'll sign if I sign first?

CLARK. Well, how do I know *you'll* sign if *I* sign first?

BARBARA. Stop it! You can sign at the same time! (*SHE rushes to the desk, grabs another pen, and holds it out to Hamilton.*) I'll count to three, all right?

CLARK. Okay. I guess that's fair.

(Pause.)

BARBARA. Hamilton?

HAMILTON. (*Taking the pen.*) Yes, yes, all right.

BARBARA. Good. One ...

(HAMILTON and CLARK glare at each other, pens poised.)

BARBARA. Two ...

(HAMILTON and CLARK continue to glare at each other, like two gunfighters about to draw.)

BARBARA. Three ...

(HAMILTON and CLARK sign their respective papers slowly, never taking their eyes off one another. When they are finished, BARBARA heaves a sigh of relief.)

BARBARA. Good.

(SHE takes the agreement from Hamilton, looks at the signature, and delivers it to Clark. SHE takes the confession from Clark and starts toward Hamilton.

When SHE reaches the bottom of the stairs, SHE stops abruptly. SHE takes a long look at Hamilton, then takes a lighter from the bar and sets the confession on fire. SHE puts it in a large ashtray on the bar and watches it burn.)

HAMILTON. Barbara? Stop! What are you doing?

CLARK. Extreme closeup of Hamilton's panicked face! Cut to signature on the agreement in Clark's hand! Freeze frame! Slow fade to black; music up; roll credits! Okay, everybody, that's a wrap! Let's go home.

HAMILTON. What? What's going on? Barbara?

SHERIFF. (*Pokes his head in the window by the front door.*) Is that it?

BARBARA. That's it!

HAMILTON. WHAT THE HELL IS GOING ON???

SHERIFF. (*Bursts in the front door, barely able to contain his excitement.*) How'd I do? How'd I do?

BARBARA. (*Hugging him.*) You were incredible. Absolutely incredible!

SHERIFF. Can I be in your movie? Did I get the part?

CLARK. (*Unhooks his handcuffs and goes to shake the sheriff's hand.*) Absolutely! No question about it.

HAMILTON. What? How did he do that? WILL SOMEBODY TELL ME WHAT THE HELL IS GOING ON???

(HAMILTON tugs furiously at his own handcuffs. The following scene has a general feeling of celebration from everyone but Hamilton.)

BARBARA. Hamilton, relax, you'll have a stroke. Yours are real. Darling, I'd like you to meet Sheriff LeRoy Lumpkin, an extraordinary law enforcement official and, undoubtedly, the finest local actor in Harrison County, Mississippi. Wasn't he brilliant?

SHERIFF. Aww, this was nothing. You should have seen me do Starbuck last year in Biloxi …

HAMILTON. What? Starbuck??

CLARK. Hamilton! Don't you get it? You just signed away your future. Sheriff Lumpkin was working with *us* all along.

HAMILTON. "Us"? What "us"? Barbara …

BARBARA. That's right, Hamilton. Us. Me and Clark. Me and the man who appreciates me and loves me for who I am. Your lawyer will be hearing from my lawyer.

HAMILTON. But he threw you out ... after his suicide attempt ...

CLARK. No, Hamilton, I never threw her out, and I never will. All that was part of our plan. To get you out of our lives and get your filthy hands off my work.

HAMILTON. *Your* plan??? What about *my* plan? This was all my idea!

BARBARA. No it wasn't, darling. I led you through the whole thing. You know, it's really not that difficult to convince a man like you he's in control …

HAMILTON. But Derek! He's a star! He can't just disappear! You can't cover up murder, no matter how corrupt your local thespian accomplice here is!

SHERIFF. Hey! Hey! Hey! As far as I'm concerned, this was just a little practical joke to give a smart alecky big shot his comeuppance. But if you want to get serious, here, we can talk about conspiracy on *your* part to commit a felony!

HAMILTON. Conspiracy? I'm talking murder one! I'm talking dead body! I'm talking about the cold blooded shooting of the late Derek Coburn!

(Suddenly DEREK bursts through the front door. HAMILTON screams as though he is seeing Banquo's ghost.)

DEREK. Yo, dudes!
HAMILTON. Aaahhh! Aaahhh! Aaahhh!
DEREK. We got it! We got it!
HAMILTON. Aaaahhhh!
CLARK. Putnam?
DEREK. Yep!
CLARK. And Sir Cecil?
DEREK. Yep! Green light! Green light!
CLARK. Woooo! Champagne! Champagne!
SHERIFF. I'll get it. Know right where it is. Be right back.

(The SHERIFF hurries off to the kitchen. HAMILTON stares at Derek, his eyes wide.)

DEREK. Hey, Ham. How was I? It was fun to play dead.

(DEREK whips the engraved revolver—Pistol #2—out of his belt and puts it to his temple. CLARK rushes to him and snatches it away before he can pull the trigger.)

CLARK. And you were *very* good.
HAMILTON. (*Stammering.*) How ... how ... what ...

CLARK. It's really all very simple, Hamilton. When I saw what you'd done to our first film and ran screaming into the night, I didn't really try to kill myself. Actually, I thought very seriously of killing *you*!

(HE points pistol at Hamilton; HAMILTON reacts.)

CLARK. But I'm not insane. And I'm not a murderer. (*During the following, HE replaces the pistol in the governor's case.*) So when Barbara came after me, we began to make a plan. It took us six months to work out all the details, and another six for Barbara to work on you, so you'd think you were in charge.

HAMILTON. But Derek—he should be dead! The bullet ... the one *after* the dud I planted ...

CLARK. (*Interrupting.*) Was a *blank*.

HAMILTON. But how...??

BARBARA. (*Suddenly pounds on an imaginary door.*) Darling! Let me in! I'm cold!

CLARK. (*Imitating Hamilton.*) Barbara! Too soon! Too soon! Not yet.

DEREK. No booze in the kitchen, man ... wooo, it's like a Safeway in there.

CLARK. (*Imitating Hamilton.*) Derek! Go back! Go away!

BARBARA. Hamilton! Let me in!

CLARK. (*As himself, frantic.*) Hamilton, give me the gun! Go to the door! I can load it! (*Then triumphantly.*) ...with a *blank*. I thought the blood looked very real, didn't you? Barbara, we really must send a note to the people in special effects.

HAMILTON. And Derek went along...?

BARBARA. (*Goes to Derek, kisses his cheek.*) Derek was a doll, darling. You see, when we told him that Bill Putnam really wanted to do Clark's script, he got very excited and went straight to Pegasus ... Derek will be playing *Cousin* Norton now.

HAMILTON. *Cousin* Norton? Derek gave up top billing to play *Cousin* Norton???

DEREK. Oh, man, a shot at working with "The Putt"? And the big Sir C? What can I say?

HAMILTON. Sir C?

CLARK. Yes, Hamilton. Cecil Harrington. He'll be directing *Return to Vicksburg*, now that you've so graciously withdrawn from participation. He's *very* good. And, Hamilton? Come next April ... I'm thinking of a little gold statue whose name begins with "O."

SHERIFF. (*Returns from the kitchen, wheeling a serving cart with champagne on ice and a number of cups.*) Bubbly, bubbly, bubbly. Sort of early in the day for me, but ... what the hell! Can you get this open while I pass out some cups?

CLARK. Certainly.

(HE hands Clark the bottle. CLARK begins to work on the cork. The SHERIFF begins passing around cups.)

HAMILTON. Wait a minute! Stop! STOP IT!

(EVERYONE stops and turns to Hamilton.)

HAMILTON. This is all very clever. I applaud your ingenuity. But you can't really hope to get away with it.

That ... that paper. Clark's no lawyer. It has to be full of more loopholes than ....

BARBARA. I don't think so, darling. It was drawn up three months ago in Hollywood by Franklin, Feinstein, Rodriguez, and Woo.

(HAMILTON reacts. BARBARA begins to laugh.)

BARBARA. Did you really think Clark banged it out on the sheriff's old Olivetti?

HAMILTON. But it isn't witnessed! It isn't notarized!

(The SHERIFF takes a notary stamp from his pocket, takes the paper from Clark and stamps it.)

SHERIFF. It is now.

(BARBARA and DEREK applaud. At that moment, CLARK pops the cork on the bottle. Champagne spews everywhere. CLARK, BARBARA, and DEREK cheer; the SHERIFF runs over with cups and tries to keep the champagne from spilling on the carpet.)

SHERIFF. Oh, my lord, what a mess. We're going to be up all night cleaning this place. Listen, would you folks mind if we moved our little party out of Skippy's living room? I mean, we could go over to the jail, or to my place, or even just down to the beach ...

DEREK. (*Chanting.*) The beach! The beach!

CLARK.	BARBARA.
The beach!	The beach!

SHERIFF. The beach it is.

(DEREK and the SHERIFF each grab a bottle of champagne. BARBARA and CLARK take cups, ice bucket, etc.)

DEREK. Did you really play Starbuck?

HAMILTON. Barbara?

SHERIFF. Oh, yes. I sure did.

HAMILTON. Barbara!

SHERIFF. Played Willie Loman once, too.

DEREK. Yeah?

HAMILTON. (*Rattling his handcuffs.*) Sheriff!!!

SHERIFF. (*To Hamilton, dismissing.*) I'll be back for you. (*To Derek.*) I liked Starbuck better. (*And THEY are out the door.*)

HAMILTON. (*Calling after them.*) Sheriff???

(CLARK and BARBARA are about to follow them. CLARK holds the door for her. HAMILTON calls out sharply.)

HAMILTON. Barbara! Come back here!

(BARBARA freezes, then turns slowly to face Hamilton.)

HAMILTON. You're not really going to do this to me.

BARBARA. Hamilton. Let's say your life is a movie. It's flashy. Fast paced. Good supporting cast. Potentially ... a great success. But if your script has no joy, no love, no compassion—*no* one will stay to see how it ends. So after the big chase, when the music plays and the lights come up—the movie house will be empty.

(SHE turns and walks to the door. SHE and CLARK are about to exit when CLARK stops and turns to Hamilton. HE looks at him for a moment, then walks to the piano and switches it on.

Honky Tonk piano MUSIC fills the room. BARBARA and CLARK exit together, leaving Hamilton alone as the LIGHTS go down and the MUSIC fills the theatre.)

THE END

PLAYWRIGHTS' NOTES

The Pistols

In the interests of safety and simplicity, the playwrights suggest the following procedure for use of the commemorative pistols:

1. There should be *three* identical commemorative pistols, only one of which is capable of firing.

2. The "live" commemorative pistol should be fully loaded with blanks before the opening curtain and pre-set under the desk.

3. The two non-firing commemorative pistols should be used throughout the first act *until* the point in the script at which Clark crawls under the desk to "load" the pistol for the replay of the suicide scene. At this point, Clark should simply exchange the non-firing pistol for the pre-set loaded pistol, which will fire the blank at the end of the act.

If this procedure is followed, the "live" pistol is actually used onstage only for the final moments of Act I, and the risk of confusion and accidental firing during the earlier scenes is eliminated.

For additional safety, we suggest the use of theatrical quarter or half-load, no wad/no paint, crimped blanks, such as those available from Centre Firearms in New York City.

The Piano Music

As for the player piano music used in the show, the authors request that the music of Scott Joplin *not* be used, as Mr. Joplin's music has become so closely associated in the public mind with the film, *The Sting*. As the plot of our play hinges on a "sting" operation as well, such an association for the audience before the final revelations would be unfortunate.

The Fireplace

If it is impossible to include a working fireplace in the set, we suggest that Hamilton simply drop the paper he burns before Clark's first entrance in a fireproof wastebasket beside the desk, and that there be a large ashtray on the bar which Barbara can use for the burning of Clark's confession in Act II.

The Handcuffs

Finally, there is the question of the handcuffs. Depending on the configuration of the set, Hamilton and Clark may be handcuffed to any available railing, handle, banister, drawer pull, etc.; as long as there is considerable separation between them for their verbal confrontations in Act II.

COSTUME PLOT

ACT I

Hamilton:
Long-sleeved solid color silk shirt
Linen trousers
Italian loafers
Handkerchief (in trousers pocket)

Barbara:
First entrance:
Tailored silk or linen suit
Silk blouse
Low-heeled pumps
Second entrance:
Bathing suit with sarong
Sandals
Beach jacket

Clark:
Hawaiian shirt
Bermuda shorts
Calf-high white socks
Sneakers or sandals

Derek:
First entrance:
Tank top
Brightly colored floral shirt, open
Draw-string cotton or linen pants
Sandals

Changes to:
Baggy swim trunks
Changes to:
Second tank top (light color)
Designer jump suit

ACT II

Scene 1

Sheriff:
Khaki sheriff's uniform with badge and arm patches
Gun belt with holster, two handcuff cases, flashlight

Barbara:
Casual slacks over Act I costume

Hamilton and Clark:
Same as Act I

Scene 2

Hamilton:
Silk pajamas
Full-length robe
Bedroom slippers

Sheriff:
Olive green or brown gardening overalls
Plaid flannel shirt
Work boots
Gun belt with pistol and handcuffs (from Scene l)

Barbara:
Short night gown

Silk dressing gown
Slippers

Derek:
Blood-stained tank top (identical to Act I)
Draw-string pants
Sandals

Clark:
Same as Act I

PROPERTY PLOT

ACT I

On Stage:

On the desk:

Cardboard boxes
Four packages of Fig Newtons
Laptop computer with disk drive
Computer disk (in disk drive of computer)
Small printer
Screenplay manuscript: "Return to Vicksburg"
Computer paper
Pencils and pens

On the bar:

Large ashtray
Cigarette lighter
Ice bucket with ice
Ice tongs
Liter of Russian vodka
Various glasses

In the oak gun case:

Several rifles and shotguns, including 12 gauge double barrel shotgun
.38 caliber pistol (in drawer)
Box of ammunition for commemorative pistols containing a half dozen "dummy" shells (in drawer)

In the pistol display case:

Two identical commemorative revolvers (Pistol #1 and Pistol #2—Pistol #2 contains the "dud" shell)

Under the desk:
"Live" commemorative pistol (see Playwrights' Notes)

In the room:
More cardboard boxes
Fireproof wastebasket
Piano rolls (on piano)

Offstage (kitchen):
Large jar of pickled plums
Half-gallon bottle of bourbon

Personal:

Hamilton:
Watch
Cigarette lighter
Handkerchief

Barbara:
Her luggage (Carry-on bag and one piece of hand luggage)
Derek's luggage (Large blue bag, suit bag, two other travel bags—blue bag contains: Swim trunks, cocaine vial, and jump suit for onstage costume change after second entrance)
Sunglasses
Copy of Premiere Magazine (for 2nd entrance)
Towel (for 2nd entrance)

Clark:
Small suitcase

Folder containing several newspaper clippings preserved in plastic (pre-set in suitcase)

ACT II

Scene 1

On Stage:
Large Porky Pig beach blanket (covering Clark)

Offstage (kitchen):
Jar of green tomato pickles

Personal:

Sheriff:
Pocket sized notebook
Pencil
Police revolver loaded with blanks
Two sets of handcuffs (on gun belt)

Barbara:
Computer disk (in pocket of beach jacket)

Scene 2

On Stage:
Empty champagne bottles
Champagne glasses

Offstage (kitchen):
Serving tray

Coffee service (Coffee pot, cups, spoons, saucers, creamer, sugar bowl, spoons)

Serving cart with:

Two bottles of champagne

Ice bucket with ice

Small bar towel

Cups

Personal:

Sheriff:

Notebook and pencil (from Scene I)

Business cards

Pocket watch

Typewritten confession

Notary stamp

Barbara:

Kleenex (for second entrance)

Clark:

Typewritten agreement

Derek:

Pistol #2 (from Act I)

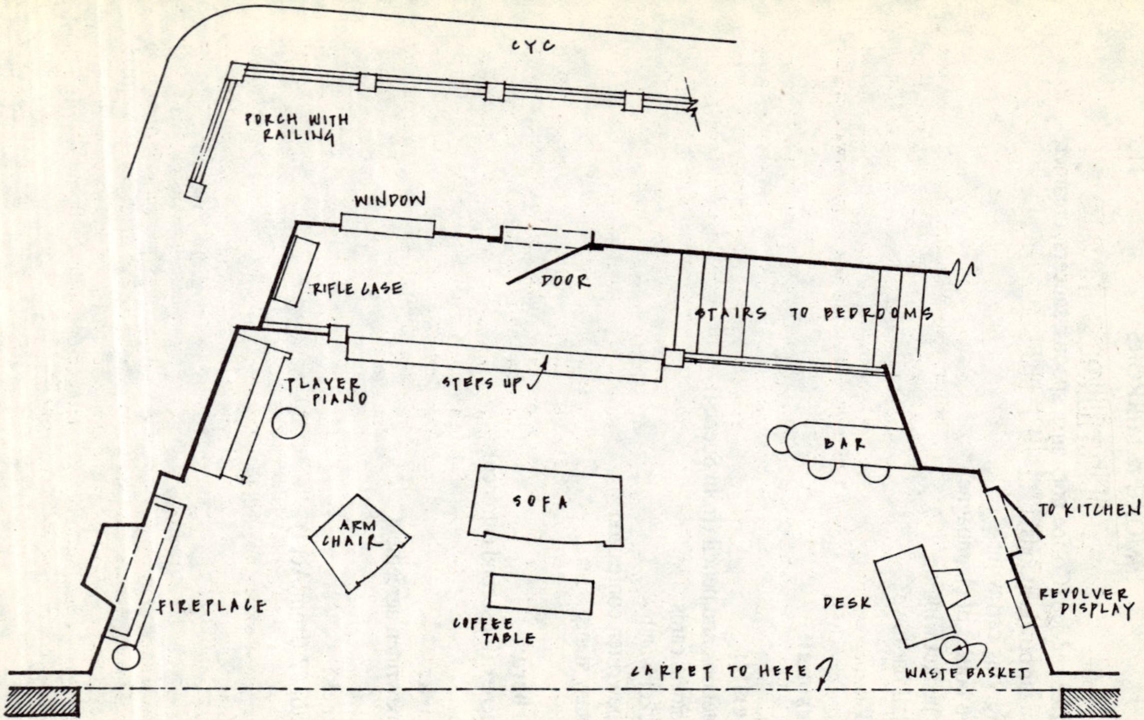

SMOKE & MIRRORS GROUNDPLAN

New Thrillers from Samuel French, Inc.

ACCOMPLICE. (Little Theatre). Thriller. Rupert Holmes. 2m., 2f., plus one surprise guest star. Int. This truly unique new thriller by the author *The Mystery of Edwin Drood* broke all box office records at the Pasadena Playhouse, and went on to thrill audiences on Broadway. Sorry, but the only way we can describe the amazing plot for you is to "give it away." *Accomplice* starts out as a straightforward English thriller, set in a country house, in which a sex-starved wife plans, with the help of her lover, to murder her stuffy husband. All is, of course, not as it first seems. Oh, yes!—the "husband" is murdered onstage; but, later, he re-enters! Why? Because what we have actually been watching is a dress rehearsal. The play takes a new twist when we learn that this is an out-of-town tryout. The "husband" we have just seen "murdered" is actually the playwright and director of the play-within-the-play, and *he* has plotted to murder his *wife*, the actress playing the lead in his play, so that he can proceed unimpeded with his affair with her leading man. Got that so far? Well—you ain't seen *nothing* yet! A surprise character comes out of the audience (no—we won't tell you who it is), revealing that, in actuality, something entirely different is going on. A cast member is being set up—brilliantly and effectively, it turns out; and the cast has its final revenge against a fellow thespian whose cruelty resulted in the suicide of a friend. "The show is a delight. It is humorous, odd, scary, wildly dramatic, adult, adolescent—in short, impossible to dislike."—Pasadena Star-News. "Miss it at your peril."—L.A. Herald Examiner. "Wonderfully entertaining . . . a breathless ride through an ever-shifting series of planes."—Cleveland Plain Dealer. "A total delight."—Bergen News. "Part murder mystery, part sex farce and completely entertaining . . . suspenseful, charming and funny."—USA Today. Slightly restricted. **(#3144)**

MAKING A KILLING. (Little Theatre.) Thriller. John Nassivera. 2m., 2f. Comb. Int. A Broadway playwright, his conniving producer and his actress wife hatch a plot to guarantee their new play will be a success; they fake the suicide of the playwright on opening night! They then high-tail it up to Vermont where the playwright hopes to disappear, as he hates the public spotlight anyway. However, after a few weeks the playwright decides he no longer wants to participate in the scheme. Maybe his wife and his producer (who are having an affair) will have to kill him for real! Also on the scene is the playwright's feisty agent, who uncovers the plot and then helps her client deal with his most difficult artistic challenge: foiling his producer and wife! "A magnificent mystery thriller ... wonderful entertainment."—Bennington Banner. "Absorbing theatre."—Schenectady Gazette. **(#15200)**

Other Publications For Your Interest

RAVENSCROFT. (Little Theatre.) Mystery. Don Nigro. 1m., 5f. Simple unit set. This unusual play is several cuts above the genre it explores, a Gothic thriller for groups that don't usually do such things, a thinking person's mystery, a dark comedy that is at times immensely funny and at others quite frightening. On a snowy night, Inspector Ruffing is called to a remote English country house to investigate the headlong plunge of a young manservant, Patrick Roarke, down the main staircase, and finds himself getting increasingly involved in the lives of five alluring and dangerous women—Marcy, the beautiful Viennese governess with a past, Mrs. Ravenscroft, the flirtatious and chattery lady of the manor, Gillian, her charming but possibly demented daughter, Mrs. French, the formidable and passionate cook, and Dolly, a frantic and terrified little maid—who lead him through an increasingly bewildering labyrinth of contradictory versions of what happened to Patrick and to the dead Mr. Ravenscroft before him. There are ghosts at the top of the staircase, skeletons in the closet, and much more than the Inspector had bargained for as his quest to solve one mystery leads him deeper and deeper into others and to an investigation of his own tortured soul and the nature of truth itself. You will not guess the ending, but you will be teased, seduced, bewildered, amused, frightened and led along with the Inspector to a dark encounter with truth, or something even stranger. A funny, first rate psychological mystery, and more.

(#19987)

DARK SONNETS OF THE LADY, THE. (Advanced Groups.) Drama. Don Nigro. 4m., 4f. Unit set. First produced professionally at the McCarter Theatre in Princeton and a finalist for the National Play Award, this stunningly theatrical and very funny drama takes place in Vienna in the fall of the year 1900, when Dora, a beautiful and brilliant young girl, walks into the office of Sigmund Freud, then an obscure doctor in his forties, to begin the most famous and controversial encounter in the history of psychoanalysis. Dora is funny, suspicious, sarcastic and elusive, and Freud become fascinated and obsessed by her and by the intricate labyrinth of her illness. He moves like a detective through the mystery of her life, and we meet in the course of his journey through her mind: her lecherous father, her obsessively house-cleaning mother, her irritating brother, her sinister admirer Herr Klippstein and his sensual and seductive wife, and their pretty and lost little governess. Nightmares, fantasies, hallucinations and memories all come alive onstage in a wild kaleidoscopic tapestry as Freud moves closer and closer to the truth about Dora's murky past, and the play becomes a kind of war between the two of them about what the truth is, about the uneasy truce between men and women, and ultimately a tragic love story. Laced throughout with eerie and haunting Strauss waltzes, this is a rich, complex, challenging and delightfully intriguing universe, a series of riddles one inside the other that lead the audience step by step to the center of Dora's troubled soul and her innermost secrets. Is Dora sick, or is the corrupt patriarchal society in which she and Freud are both trapped the real source of a complex group neurosis that binds all the characters together in a dark web of desperate erotic relationships, a kind of beautiful, insane and terrible dance of life, desire and death?

(#5952)

Other publications for your interest:

SULLIVAN AND GILBERT

(Little Theatre/Musical)
by Ken Ludwig
music by Sir Arthur Sullivan
lyrics by William S. Gilbert

8 male, 4 female, Ints.

Gilbert & Sullivan created some of the world's best-loved musical theatre; but they did not make beautiful music together. Eventually their collaboration ended, riven by Sullivan's chafing at Gilbert's pretensions as a "serious poet" and Gilbert's jealousy over the fact that Sullivan had been knighted and he hadn't. In 1890 Gilbert and Sullivan, who have been at each other's throats for years, are forced to work together one more time: Queen Victoria has requested a command performance of their most popular songs. So, they are putting together a revue of, well--Gilbert & Sullivan's Greatest Hits, complicated by the presence of Arthur, Duke of Edinburgh, son of Queen Victoria, whom Sullivan has agreed to allow to perform in the show, *much* to the consternation of Gilbert, who considers the Duke to be a "dumbbell with a title". Also present is Richard D'Oyly Carte, valiantly trying to mediate, as well as the principal Savoyards of the day, who perform delightfully songs from *The Mikado, Ruddigore,, Iolanthe, Princess Ida, H.M.S. Pinafore, Patience* and *The Pirates of Penzance*. "A charming show."--Boston Globe. Music on rental. #21385

THE NIGHT HANK WILLIAMS DIED

(Little Theatre)
(COMIC/DRAMA)
by Larry L. King

4 male, 2 female, Int.

Thurmond Stottle, once the local high school football hero, is reduced to pumping gas at the local Gulf Station in the tiny West Texas town of Stanley. Thurmond has big dreams, though--he wants to make it as a songwriter and country singer like his hero, the late Hank Williams. He whiles away his free time hanging out in the local bar run by Gus Gilbert, on whom he tries out his latest tunes, and waits for the right moment to take off for Nashville. The moment arrives along with Nellie Bess Powers Clark, his ex-high school sweetheart, who has returned home as her marriage is breaking up. Nellie and Thurmond re-kindle the old flames, and Thurmond plans to leave for Nashville with Nellie--if he can get a stake from Gus. When Gus turns him down, he does a very foolish thing: he robs the gas station, bludgeoning the owner. He returns to Gus' bar to hide and decide what to do; but the sheriff knows just where to find him . . . "A wistful yet mordant folk play. Its theme ...is timeless."--Chr. Sc. Mon. "The plot is strong, and there is no lack of incident or characters, but it is the rich Texas vernacular--the rat-tat-tat of startling, bawdy similes and the funny throwaway lines--that gives the show its texture."--New Yorker. "Amusing and ultimately poignant. A fine, new play "--N.Y. Times. Write for details about music. #15989

Other Publications for Your Interest

CAT'S PAW

(LITTLE THEATRE—DRAMA)

By WILLIAM MASTROSIMONE

2 men, 2 women—Interior

This is a gripping drama about terrorism; but it does not come at the subject in a way you'd expect. When we think of "the terrorist", we generally think of a wild-eyed religious or political fanatic. What if, posits the acclaimed author of *The Woolgatherer*, *Extremities*, *Shivaree* and *Nanawatai*, a terrorist came along who was brilliant, who was articulate and who was *right*? Victor is the head of a terrorist group which is responsible for a bomb attack against the White House in which 27 people have been killed. He has arranged to have a television news reporter led to his lair, there to tell the world why he has done what he has done. Victor's obsession is the destruction of the world's water supply, and with it the final destruction of the human race, by pollution. When the reporter asks him if he feels any guilt about the death of the 27 innocent people, he replies that hundreds of innocent people are dying every hour because of what mankind is doing to its water supply—and do the people responsible feel guilt for this? This cat-and-mouse game between the young woman reporter and Victor gets more and more tense, leading to a shocking and violent conclusion. A standing-room-only hit at Seattle Repertory Theatre and later at San Diego's Old Globe. "An agonizingly suspenseful thriller."—San Diego Tribune. "A grabber."—Seattle Times. "Timely, thought-provoking and definitely worth seeing."—San Diego Reader. "Entertaining, informative, thoughtful and scary."—The Weekly (Seattle). (#5056)

SHIVAREE

(LITTLE THEATRE—COMIC DRAMA)

By WILLIAM MASTROSIMONE

2 men, 3 women—Combination interior

We are delighted to publish this lesser-known but wonderful play by the acclaimed author of *Extremities* and *The Woolgatherer*. The story concerns a young hemophiliac youth named Chandler who has been kept, of necessity, by his cab driver mother in a very sheltered sort of existence. Chandler is desperate for contact with the world. He is also highly intelligent; but is supremely naive about the ways of the world. He pays a neighbor to bring him a girl; but he can't go through with his plans to have sex with her. He just doesn't know what to do about his craving for love—until he meets Shivaree. She is another neighbor who supports herself by being an itinerant belly-dancer. She is a True Original, and before too long the delightful Shivaree and the innocent Chandler are in love, much to the consternation of Chandler's mother, who forbids Chandler to ever see Shivaree again, throwing Shivaree out of Chandler's room. Chandler, undaunted, climbs out the fire escape—his first venture outside his hermetic world—going after his love. Fans of Mr. Mastrosimone's other plays will recognize the true-ness of the characterizations and the poignancy and humor of typical Mastrosimone dialogue in this wonderful play. (#21689)

FAVORITE MELODRAMAS

VIRTUE ALWAYS TRIUMPHS; or LIFE IN THE WICKED CITY. (Little Theatre.) Melodrama. Walter Boughton. 14m., 5f. (doubling possible). 3 ints. A damsel in distress named Charity takes refuge in Amos Truhart's house during a raging blizzard. She is trying to escape the clutches of the perfidious Warrington Chadbourne, after her because she is the sole heir to a huge railroad fortune. Chadbourne wants to marry her and then do her in for the money. While staying with the Truharts, Charity falls in love with their son, Tyrone, who forthwith proposes that they tie the nuptial knot; but Charity has a sordid past (so she thinks), so she declines. Our hero, Tyrone Truhart, is indefatigable in his devotion to Charity, even when Chadbourne frames Charity on a charge of having borne an illegitimate child. Charity leaves with the child and winds up on the Bowery, pursued hotly by Tyrone, who wants to rescue her and clear her name, and Chadbourne, who only cares about her money. Chadbourne finds her first, and threatens to kill the child unless she marries him. Will Tyrone come to the rescue in time? *Is* Charity the daughter of Slick Annie, the Fence, or someone else entirely? Well, to find out you'll just have to order a copy of this delightful, fast-paced new old-time "mellerdrammer." **(#24617)**

SAY UNCLE, UNCLE SILAS. (Trapped in a House of Fiends) (All Groups.) Melodrama Spoof. Tim Kelly. 9f., 5m. Simple Staging. Savage murders! Blackmail! Thunderstorms! Chewed scenery! And yes—romance! This is an hilarious laff-a-minute spoof of English Gothic melodramas. Suggested by Sheridan LeFanu's *Uncle Silas*. The setting is Barnum-Hogg, a grim edifice that looks like Wuthering Heights after a fire. Ghosts walk and tombstones in the graveyard "stick up like swollen thumbs." Enter Maud Ruthyn, a young heiress who'll remind you of Jane Eyre on a bad day. She soon finds herself menaced by her creepy relative who makes Sweeney Todd seem like a nice guy. To tutor our heroine he hires a monstrous governess, Madame De La Rougepot. Silas hopes to force Maud to marry his brute of a son, Dudley. However, Dudley has a secret wife! Silas formulates another plan to get Maud's fortune. It's a very nasty (and uproarious) scheme involving deception, deceit and more murder. Horrors! Will handsome Captain Oakley and sophisticated Lady Monica save Maud in time? Will the mystery of the locked room be revealed? Said one reviewer, "Subtle it's not, funny it is." Bad acting and cheap scenery can only help. Wonderfully goofy roles and no production hassles. An audience and cast pleaser. By the author of *Egad, The Woman in White* and *The Face on the Barroom Floor*. **(#20995)**

Other Publications For Your Interest

PICTURE OF DORIAN GRAY, THE. (Little Theatre.) Drama. Adapted by John Osborne from the novel by Oscar Wilde. 11m., 4f., plus extras. I Int. w/apron for other scenes. English playwright John Osborne (Look Back in Anger, Inadmissible Evidence, The Entertainer) has given us a brilliant dramatisation of Wilde's classic novel about a young man who, magically, retains his youth and beauty while the decay of advancing years and moral corruption only appears on a portrait painted by one of his lovers. Following the advice of the evil Lord Harry, a cynic who, fashionably, mocks any and all institutions and moral precepts, Dorian comes to believe that the only purpose of life is simply for one to realize, and glorify, one's own nature. In so doing, he is inevitably sucked into the maelstrom of degradation and despair, human nature being what it is. "Osborne has done much more than a scissors-and-paste job on Wilde's famous story. He has thinned out the over-abundant epigrams, he has highlighted the topical concept of youth as a commodity for which one would sell one's soul and he has, in Turn of the Screw fashion, created a sense of evil through implication. Osborne conveys moral disintegration through the gradual breakdown of the hero's language into terse, broken phrases and through a creeping phantasmagoria."—London, The Guardian. "What is so interesting about John Osborne's adaptation of The Picture of Dorian Gray is that he had found in Oscar Wilde's macabre morality a velveted barouche for his own favorite themes. Osborne funks none of the greenery-valley vulgarity of the fabulous story, and conveys much of its fascination."—London, Daily Telegraph. State author when ordering. **(#18954)**

FALL OF THE HOUSE OF USHER, THE. (Little Theatre.) Drama. Gip Hoppe. Music by Jay Hagenbuckle. 6m. 3f. Int. A comfortable suburban family man receives a desperate telephone call from an obscure and forgotten childhood acquaintance. Thus starts a journey into madness that will take Ed Allen to the House of Usher and the terrible secrets and temptations contained there. In this modern adaptation of the classic short story by Edgar Allen Poe, playwright Gip Hoppe takes Gothic horror into the 90s, questioning the definition of "sanity" in the same way Poe did in his day. Ed arrives to find Roderick in a state of panic and anxiety over the impending death of his sister, Madeline. As he tries to sort out the facts, he becomes tangled in a family web of incest and murder. Finding himself infatuated with the beautiful Madeline, his "outside life" fades from his memory as he descends to the depths of madness that inflict all the residents of The House of Usher. *The Fall of the House of Usher* is an exhilarating theatrical adventure leading to an apocalyptic ending that will have audiences thrilled. Actors and designers will be challenged in new ways in this unpredictable and wildly entertaining play. Cassette tape. Use of Mr. Hagenbuckle's music will greatly enhance the play, but it is not mandatory. **(#7991)**